This small book is on the impending and unprecedented glorious Golden Age of Peace about to dawn upon the whole world (and on how you can help bring about its arrival quickly). An eBook and an audiobook are available at www.CrownOfHistory.com, where inquiries may also be made regarding discounted bulk orders of the paperback. *The Crown of Sanctity*, referenced throughout the forthcoming pages, is available for free at www.CrownOfSanctity.com.

Published on the Feast of the Triumph of the Cross: September 14, 2019.

†‡†

Brief Contents

†‡†

I) The Story of History

Once upon a time before time, there was nothing—nothing but God. Then, in a plan of pure love (for being infinitely perfect, the Creator needs nothing and cannot act from ulterior motives), He deigned to create a world. Although He promptly filled it with beings that glorified (in the beauty proper to the nature of each) some attribute of His, this world that He so loved could not yet receive all of His love, for He saw that it lacked only one thing. Thus, disregarding that terrible but tempting advice one often hears, "safety first," He chose to create other beings like Himself—made in His own Image and Likeness with an intellect, memory, and will—who, as a consequence of their innate abilities, could choose either to love their Father and Creator, or to rebel against Him.

The rest is history. But history, indeed, as has often been rightly said, is *His* Story—the story that God Himself is telling through His Providential direction of all things. For He charts the course of the stars, the growth of the plants, and the instincts of the animals with the direct exercise of His dominion just as any author traces the curves of each letter with ink upon a page, but He serves as the Architect of History in an altogether different way in the midst of His greatest handiwork: human beings. With us, His task is infinitely more difficult; and, as we shall see upon the commencement of the fruition of His plan, infinitely more beautiful. For in creating us in His Image, He has given us the ability (and the *need*) to possess His very life as our own life.

But we do *not* possess His life as our own life. For whatever your religion or other ideological persuasion, you know full well—in your heart of hearts, if nowhere else—that the world is simply not the way it should be, nor, indeed, is your own life.

Thankfully, this apparently sorry state is not so sorrowful after all: for God, as the author of History, is not lacking in the same wisdom that the greatest human authors possess. And all such human authors know that the greatest stories require five essential elements. *Once upon a time...*

1. **The Exposition:** The setting is laid out—*how things ought to be* is made clear.
2. **The Rising Action:** The antagonist enters, the conflict begins, *how things ought to be* becomes distorted, and matters grow ever more serious.
3. **The Climax:** The tides have turned, the main event has transpired, and the protagonist *embarks* upon the path of his eventual victory.
4. **The Falling Action:** The conflict begins to be resolved; there is much striving—many triumphs, but also failures—it is at once glorious and painful, and though the process has begun, *how things ought to be* has not yet been fully restored.
5. **The Dénouement:** The conflict is resolved. The setting in the Exposition is not only restored, but the protagonist is even more blessed than in the Exposition.

And then, there must be the *Happily Ever After.*

Consider how beautifully J.R.R. Tolkien's *The Lord of the Rings* displays the symmetry of this dramatic structure; beginning, as it does, in the green and peaceful land of the Shire, only to return to this same setting after the great adventure, the tremendous trial, the vanquishing of the evil antagonist, and the initiation of the Days of Peace. Likewise, Alexander Dumas' *The Count of Monte Cristo* begins with the blissful lives of the betrothed Edmond Dantès and Mercédès, only to return to this bliss after enormous trials, with the final words of the story reminding us that, "*all human wisdom is summed up in these two words, 'Wait and Hope.'*" And no admonition could be more germane to the matter at hand, for throughout the pages now before you, it will become apparent that God, as the Greatest Author, will not fail to ensure that His own story contains the essential elements and symmetry of any good story. Now, in the story that is history, God already has led us through the first four elements:

1. **The Exposition.** In the Garden of Eden, God showed us His original plan: everything good, everything beautiful, everything perfect. The lion's teeth serving not to tear apart flesh, but rather to glorify God's strength. Man himself living as a being of such glory as to astonish the angels themselves. The whole earth destined to be filled with people living in perfect peace and harmony with one another and with all creation, each living a long and happy life until his own time came to painlessly depart for his true, *eternal* home: Heaven.
2. **The Rising Action.** Beginning with the Fall of Man by Adam's failure to pass God's simple test of love and the resulting emergence of sin, death, suffering, and ugliness—the world became more and more corrupt; needing, at one point, to even be purged by a universal flood. But God had His chosen people, and within this people, a remnant never forgot that He had promised the Redeemer. These faithful Israelites, in accordance with their sure and certain hope, always prayed in earnest that the Messiah would come to save mankind.
3. **The Climax.** When the fullness of time had arrived, God deigned to create a creature

unlike any that had existed before: *The* Woman whom He had promised 4,000 years earlier, whose seed would crush the serpent (Genesis 3:15). This woman, reversing Adam's disobedience, gave her *Fiat* to God when He asked permission for her to become His own true mother. Nine months later, laid in a manger, the Creator of the Universe was worshipped by Kings and shepherds alike. This man, Jesus Christ, founded a Church, willingly handed over His life for our salvation and sanctification, rose from the dead to abolish doubt forever, and ascended to Heaven.

4. **The Falling Action.** For 2,000 years, His Gospel has been tirelessly preached and lived in ever-growing nations and numbers. The saints throughout this time have lived this Gospel—often perfectly—and have both filled the earth with His Love and populated Heaven with their children.

But, great and glorious as the many triumphs of the Church and the saints have been, only a willfully blind man could argue that the Kingdom of God now reigns on earth to the extent that God wills and to the extent that God has promised in His prayer "*Thy Kingdom come, Thy Will be done, on earth as it is in Heaven.*" (Matthew 6:10) Some Christians today propose that this fourth element is all the earth will ever see—that in Heaven alone could anyone ever hope to experience The Dénouement. But that is not what Jesus said, it is not what the Church teaches (see the appendices), it is not what virtually all the Fathers of the Church believed, and it is not what God has spoken to the Church today through the unanimous consensus of His chosen—and proven—prophets (all of which we will see shortly in Chapter I). Heaven is our *happily ever after.* But Heaven is not *within* the Story of History—Heaven is the *purpose* of this story and dwells beyond its pages. For the Story of History to be complete, like any story, its *own* pages must contain The Dénouement.

5. **The Dénouement:** You, dear reader, have been blessed to be born in the most exciting part of The Story, for The Dénouement is now being written before your very eyes. It is *the* fulfillment. It is the granting of the greatest petition of the greatest prayer ever uttered by the lips of man: the only prayer that Jesus Himself taught us to pray, in which He promised that the Will of the Father would reign on earth just as It reigns in Heaven. But you must read on to see in what this fulfillment consists and how you can ensure it comes quickly.

†‡†

II) The Story of You: A Day in the Life of a Citizen of the Era

If I had a crystal ball, I would smash it into a thousand pieces. For what I do have— knowledge of the things the trustworthy prophecies have said about certain happenings guaranteed to soon transpire upon this world—is infinitely superior. And while some of what follows is my own educated speculation, most of it comes directly from these prophecies. Let us, then, walk through a Day in the Life of a Citizen of the Era which, please God, you yourself shall soon be. (I must warn you: I am a philosopher and an engineer—I have absolutely no ability to write fiction. Any merit in what follows, therefore, exists only by virtue of its contents being *non*-fiction.)

Opening your eyes for the first time of the new day, you are inundated—not with anxiety over what you must accomplish that day, not with physical pain, not with a miserable desire to remain sleeping and annihilate your alarm clock—but with an overwhelming sensation of joy and gratitude for life. Although it is just another "ordinary" day, you arise from bed with all the ease and excitement of a child on Christmas morning, and walking to the nearest door of your home (kept wide open, for you saw no reason to shut it—much less lock it—the night before), you gaze upon the rising of the sun and glorify the God Who made it. Though once a very "pragmatic" man who could not be bothered with mysticism, you (and all) now feel such compulsion to rejoice upon recognizing the Divinity veiled by created things that you make St. Francis of Assisi look like a bore. What you once never bothered to drag yourself out of bed to experience is now, each day, a spectacle the likes of which anyone from the former days would have eagerly spent his life savings to witness just once. For, emerging triumphantly above the horizon across your town's eastern valley, this rising sun communicates such new beauty to all the things it illuminates that its effects can only be compared to the crescendo of a classical masterpiece, and this experience is for all nothing less than an enrapturing daily preview of the Final Coming itself.

As she did before the Era, your grandmother lives in the home with your wife and children—she is one hundred and ten years old, but now rises to begin her day with no less ease and no less joy than you yourself did minutes before; her previous Alzheimer's and arthritis having vanished without a trace. Your wife and children arise in the same manner, and you all join together to continue your prayer of thanksgiving to God for another day of joy, beauty, harmony, and peace—living in His Will and in His Kingdom upon earth. Reciting this prayer with your family, you bask in such happiness that your fondest memory from the old era does not even begin to hold a candle to it. And there is not the remotest hint (nor is there ever) of the things that once robbed your home of that joy: the discord, the fighting of children, the former sinful habits of those dwelling within its walls; and gone too is any vestige of mental, emotional, and physical ailments. In the old era, all these sorry things often invaded the peace of your home; now, they are scarcely even memories—for although the mere factual recognition of their past existence has not disappeared from your mind, no morsel of the lingering hurt or nagging temptation to withhold forgiveness that memory once tended to bring with it remains. For upon the initiation of the Era, God not only miraculously cured men's wills and intellects of what they inherited from the Fall, but also their memories.

Having immensely enjoyed this time with your family, you wish to begin the rest of your day with a greater prayer still, and you walk to the nearest Church to attend Mass. During this walk, none of those unfortunate sights and sounds you once were bombarded with are anywhere to be found. No one is blaring horrendous music while driving by, as no one is driving by at all, no arguments are overheard while passing by the houses in which such occurrences once seemed perpetual, and no deafening dump trucks are passing by belching fumes. What is more, you are walking through what was once known as the "ghetto," adjacent to a heavily-used industrial park—an area where superlative chaos, noise, crime, and filth once reigned without interruption. But now, the only sounds to be heard are the prayers and loving conversations of those who live in the houses you pass and the warbling of the birds that joins in harmony with a faint and mysterious music that leaves you astounded like no orchestra in the days gone by ever did (but we will get to describing the origin of that music later).

This former ghetto—once a hideous mixture of crumbling concrete slabs, corrugated sheet metal and plywood covering windows, rotting old houses, nauseating smells, and garbage-filled streets—now more resembles what artists strive after in painting a picture of a village from a children's fantasy novel. The transformation it underwent took very little time upon the commencement of the Era, for a new family of once unknown plants exploded throughout the world like no invasive species ever could. Of enrapturing beauty and exquisite smell, these plants rapidly covered all the plastic, sheet metal, asphalt, concrete, and the like; reducing them (in a matter of days) back to stone or dirt with its roots and covering them with flowers so stunning that no gardener on earth before the Era could have hoped to so adorn his own terrace.

This daily morning walk through what is now a foretaste of Heaven soon brings you to that which is more than just a foretaste of the same. For despite the glory of the world during the Era, you ever long for your Celestial Fatherland—Heaven. This longing, far from being the painful thing that it sometimes was before the Era, is now pure joy and excitement; like that of vacationers waiting in an airport, as opposed to the longing of impoverished peoples who crave a trip somewhere nice but can scarcely imagine what one would be like. Unfortunately, I cannot within these pages successfully describe what you experience within those walls of the Church as you celebrate the Heavenly Liturgy which stands between Heaven and earth. For while the world during the Era is indeed glorious, it can at least be spoken of using our present language. But Heaven is infinitely more glorious still, and its description exceeds the capacities of human language. So the Mass during the Era can, perhaps, be described in part, and I will just say this: if, before the Era, most who attended Mass did so only while regularly glancing at their watches in hopes that it would soon be over, attending Mass during the Era is, for each and for all, the same experience that the great mystics had always described: the Sacred Mysteries scarcely veiled, and the Sacraments received not as medicine for the sick, but as food for the healthy. Consequently, not even those who in the old era had been written off as hopeless addicts now has any craving for the false and corrupt pseudo-mysticism of drug abuse that had so plagued the world, for genuine mystical experiences are now the norm, not the exception, and no one leaves Mass without tasting the enrapturing chaste ecstasy of Heaven itself.

Returning from Mass along a different route, you traverse a no less beautiful path. This time, it is one filled with people; for you wish to stop by the marketplace. There are no big-box stores and no malls, because there is no need for these things. Everything that anyone needs or even wants can be made by individual families and brought to their own stand in the marketplace. Your simple stroll through the marketplace makes the most joyful family reunion of the days before the Era look like a rather miserable affair: for now, each person—whether family, friend, or total stranger—has nothing but perfect and even overwhelming love for each other person. This love comes naturally and automatically to everyone; one need only step out of his house on any given day to enjoy most blessed society with others. You see, in these times, everyone believes the same things—the Truth. Everyone wills the same things—the Good. Everyone enjoys the same things—the Beautiful. Individual personalities and preferences are anything but gone; in fact, they flourish more than ever before. But now these differences exist in perfect harmony, as much unlike the discordant cacophony of the old era's "diversity" as the succession of notes of Mozart's symphonies are unlike the shrill shrieking of a heavy-metal band. And despite the joy of all the encounters you have with the people there far surpassing anything you experienced in the old days, there is at the same time no hint of boisterousness, debauchery, flirtatiousness, giddiness, or excess of any sort. There is good humor, indeed, and wholesome (even hearty) laughter, but it is built upon a foundation of serenity and peace that is never interrupted, and there is never any sarcasm or facetiousness to be seen or heard, as being ever keenly and palpably aware of the weight of your neighbor's glory renders such attitudes impossible.

Having dropped off at home what you needed from the marketplace and being filled to the brim and overflowing with love of God and neighbor, you now set off to walk to work in great gratitude for all you have been given. Before this Era of Peace, you worked as a security guard while attending medical school in hopes of becoming an oncologist. But neither of those professions are necessary any longer. So you are now an artist, an architect, a shipbuilder, and an explorer. The innumerable gifts God gratuitously bestowed upon the world's inhabitants upon the initiation of the Era makes this combination of professions in no way burdensome; infused knowledge immediately elevated you to an intellectual height that no scientist had ever achieved in the old era, giving you all the prerequisites necessary to create works of art far surpassing any masterpiece of Da Vinci. You became an explorer because the radical transformations that the world underwent upon the Great Upheaval that brought about the Era rendered its 126 billion acres so full of hitherto inconceivable Natural Wonders that the previous seven entries no longer qualify for the new list, which already has hundreds of entries and scarcely has begun to document what now exists. Hence, explorers are needed to lay human eyes—for the first time ever—upon the new beauties with which God filled the earth. Artists, furthermore, are needed to strive to capture what only human eyes can glean; eyes that, unlike the cameras of the days gone by, are capable of seeing not only the breathtaking external beauty of created things, but also the glory of God shining through them. This exploration, of course, is greatly aided by good ships, and you happily contribute your own efforts to this task at the nearby port.

You were not particularly strong or manually skilled in the old days, but you now can easily lift and hew even the largest wooden beams of which the ship's hull is constructed. Without the need of spending countless hours at the gym (none exist now, anyway) or endlessly obsessing over diet, the human body now naturally tends toward being what it was designed to be: a thing of great beauty, enormous strength, and perfect health. There are no noisy power tools within your reach at this port, for that is another old need that disappeared with the Era. Though it exceeds in sharpness even a surgeon's blade, a simple hand saw always holds its edge perfectly, and using it, you easily cut through a large beam in seconds. Every animal, too, is at your beck and call, ready to do whatever it can in accordance with its own God-given abilities; for now, each animal automatically behaves towards all men as even in the old era a perfectly trained dog behaved with respect to its owner.

Standing back to appreciate your work—which is now complete despite only taking a small fraction of the time a similar project would have consumed in the old days with the help of technology—you recall how much you thoroughly enjoyed the effort. Even though it is, objectively speaking, quite strenuous, your abilities are suited to it, thus rendering it no less natural than tying your shoes had always been. If someone from the old days were to have been given a glimpse of your labors, he would have marveled and said the same thing he says after watching an Olympic gymnast, "he makes those incredible tasks look so easy!"

Returning home for dinner, your plate contains no meat; neither is the blood of man nor of beast deliberately shed during the Era. But this is to no one's disappointment— the fruits, vegetables, nuts, and grains produced in superabundance by the plants that grow spontaneously in your own garden (flourishing there even in winter, which was once quite harsh where you live but now never calls for wearing more than a sweater) give such nutrition and taste as to make eating the most carefully prepared gourmet meal of filet mignon a penance in comparison. Despite a taste so exquisite that wars would have been fought over attaining it in the days gone by, you experience not the slightest desire to continue eating after you have been properly satiated, for the passions of the body—no longer the temptations they once were—now always *follow* reason (instead of combating it) and ennoble one's ability to correspond thereto.

The conversations you have with your family members over dinner, in addition to their laughter and good stories, fill you ever more with the love of God and of all His works. This perpetual filling, indeed, is a recurring theme in your life (though you never manage to fully comprehend it); you always feel filled to the brim and overflowing with God's love and yet, somehow, each new experience increases it ever more. Contemplating this great gift, you now notice the sun has begun to set beneath the peaks of the new mountain range you can observe in breathtaking clarity from your dining room window. Like flowing torrents of liquid gold, its beams of light cascade through your windows after assuming a hue more stunning still from their interaction with the abundant flora in your adjacent garden. This light never burns the skin or dazzles the eyes, for the human body is now perfectly accustomed to it. As it completes the day's course and sinks gently below the horizon, the stars soon begin to shine with a beauty that could not even be depicted by the old era's artificially colored telescope-captured images. With this beauty now on full display you begin to hear clearly what was faint earlier in the day but is now robust and utterly enchanting—the Celestial Music of the Spheres, a sound even the ancient Greek philosophers of the old era recognized in fact existed, now audible to all. Joining in chorus with it, you all recite your evening prayers which, despite none of you having any musical training (you were used to seeing people wince when you attempted to sing in the old era), make the most perfected polyphony of Palestrina sound like an elementary school band's first practice.

As you will need to depart long before dawn for your now completed ship's maiden voyage the next morning, you lovingly bid your family farewell for a time. Unlike those of the old era, this farewell is shrouded with no sorrow. For in the days gone by, even the best farewells were tinged with doubts and fears: *"Shall I see them again? What if I or they change for the worse before our next rendezvous? What might I miss out on? How will we bear this time apart?"* And, in an effort to battle superficially against these anxieties, a flurry of burdensome digital correspondence inevitably followed; one that neither cured the farewell of its sadness nor produced any real good for either party thereafter. But now, you haven't the faintest doubt you will see them again; neither intellectual nor emotional doubt—and if you miss them at all on your journey, it is comparable to how, before the Era, you "missed" your wife when the two of you happened to be at different ends of the table during dinner or when talking to different people at a joyful social gathering. The continuous union all experience in the Divine Will, now sensible, makes a distance of 5,000 miles feel little more than the distance of five yards, and a delay of five months little more than five minutes; furthermore, what you truly eagerly await is your Heavenly reunion with all your loved ones—a union that will infinitely outshine even the beauty of the union you enjoy with them during the Era. And there is no fear at all in your mind that any of your loved ones will not make it to their Heavenly Homeland: you are certain of seeing them there and feel this certainty within your bones; "missing" anyone, therefore, is a much different affair than it was before the Era, and no one has any desire to spend time communicating digitally with those not present before them. Transportation technologies, too, have lost all their allure. For there is no longer the frantic desire to simply arrive at numerous destinations—the adventure of the journey has reacquired its rightful place as a primary reason for each trip. This, however, is not to mention that a car would be rather superfluous on its own right; any draft horse (multitudes of them roam everywhere freely and peacefully) is now twice as fast and strong as even those which were most carefully bred and trained during the old era, in addition to sharing in the perfect obedience to man that all animals have naturally reacquired.

Deliberately omitted is a description of your travels; so glorious an adventure they are that only the likes of J.R.R. Tolkien or C.S. Lewis could hope to do them even a minimal level of justice. In the old era, you would have almost been tempted to believe someone who argued that a world without sin, error, and ugliness would be a rather boring world. Now, to even think something so preposterous would be considered blasphemous. You were indeed regularly bored mad before the Era, back when "the world was at your fingertips" due to the internet: blankly staring at a screen, not knowing what to do with yourself. Now, boredom is as foreign to you as it is to newlyweds on a long-awaited honeymoon. Epic adventures, bold conquests, enrapturing experiences, new discoveries, new friendships, and new knowledge are always immediately accessible to you now. What is more, all citizens of the Era eagerly anticipate fulfilling their own roles in that Great Final Battle they all know will immediately precede the end of time (which, for all they know, could be the next day, or the next century) when all the power of hell is briefly unleashed through Gog and Magog, and the Confrontation that follows makes all the battles in the fantastical Hollywood blockbusters, combined, look like a cheap soap opera.

Upon returning from your journey, you are the first to discover that your grandmother has died. But, although her soul did indeed depart for Heaven, its separation from her body was an event as unlike death before the Era as easing into a warm bath is unlike plunging through the sharp ice of a frozen lake. Her death would be more accurately referred to as the mere transition of her soul to its eternal home; the natural consequence of her having, at that moment, successfully completed all that God placed her on earth to accomplish. At that moment of accomplishment, her soul was so full of love and longing for a still-deeper union with its Creator that the very bonds to flesh it had hitherto enlivened were no longer strong enough to resist the pull of this love, and this same flesh readily and without a fight relinquished its rights to its own life principle.

Her body—along with those of all who die during the Era—will remain perfectly fresh in its tomb, just as it was the moment the soul departed, awaiting in perfect beauty the Day of the Resurrection and Universal Judgment at the End of Time.

Inspired beyond words by your grandmother's holy death, you look again to the setting sun as it sinks below the horizon, overwhelmed still more with joy and excitement for when your own time will come to, along with all of your loved ones, see your Creator face-to-face in the world without end.

†‡†

III) The Story of Me: A Rallying Cry from One Millennial to All

Why, dear friends, are we called Millennials? Because William Straus and Neil Howe decided it would sound good to so call those who came of age around the year 2000? Perhaps. But truly it was God, not these men, who bestowed the title. **This title belongs to us because it is our Divinely Mandated Mission to be the heralds of the Era of the Third Millennium.** I know this is my Divinely Mandated Mission, but I also know there is nothing special about me; therefore, I believe this is your mission as well.

Like many of you, I have felt from the youngest age an overpowering desire—a need, really—to save the world (it is no accident that our generation is more inundated with save-the-world movies and stories than any other). I was already in Middle School busily designing inventions that I hoped would achieve this salvation, and by High School I was prototyping them. Dedicating myself to and excelling in my studies allowed me to enroll in a top engineering University to (so was my hope) further my efforts to bring these prototypes and ideas to fruition and thereby commence my version of the transformation of the world. My first job after graduating was for GE Global Research, where I was running experiments striving for a breakthrough in generating the quantum emission of electrons off a carbon nanotube surface. But a series of pilgrimages and miraculous signs in the years leading up to that job began to teach me that the world needed much more (and much less) than I had thought; it really needed Divine Intervention, and not more technology. The ultimate wakeup call occurred the very day I became a world-record holder of sorts, having run a test resulting in the greatest quantum emission of electrons yet achieved. For, later that same day, I accepted an invitation to defend the right to life on a local radio show, and upon the day's close came the epiphany that I had done incomparably more good for the world by speaking up for Goodness and Truth than I had done by contributing to our society's further technological advancement. I was soon thereafter told by a high up GE manager that I needed to "promise to never talk about religion or politics at work again" if I were to stay on the job. Knowing that was not a promise I could in good conscience make, I walked out.

In the years that followed—and amid many adventures—I learned that the real instructions on how to save the world are found in an unlikely source: the writings of an ordinary Italian woman who died over 70 years ago. But we will get into that in the next Chapter. I now share this brief, true story about my life, in hopes that others will likewise undertake their own efforts to save the world using the most powerful and effective methods possible (methods detailed in Chapter 2).

We, dear Millennials, were born in sorry times. But it is not for us to lament the times that God chose for us before the foundation of the world. In the words of Tolkien, speaking through his greatest novel's wisest character, "**That is not for us to decide. All we have to decide is what to do with the time that is given us.**" As I write these words, the average Millennial is now about 30 years old: the same age Jesus Himself was when He left His home in Nazareth in order to proclaim the Kingdom of God. Choose your mission wisely, friends.

†‡†

Chapter I: Why Should I Believe This?

I have laid out some rather astounding truths in the preceding pages, and some readers must now have no small degree of skepticism arising in their minds. So, let us turn to consider why it is not only reasonable, but *rationally necessary*, to banish this skepticism.

Everyone Already Knows It's True

Towards the beginning of the 20th century, Jesus gave the following prophecy to a certain woman named Luisa (we will discuss this incredible person more later):

> The whole world is upside down, and everyone is awaiting changes, peace, new things. … peoples are impoverished, are stripped alive, and while they are waiting, tired of the sad present era, dark and bloody, which enwraps them, they wait and hope for a new era of peace and of light. **The world is exactly at the same point as when I was about to come upon earth. All were awaiting a great event, a new era, as indeed occurred. The same now; since the great event, the new era in which the Will of God may be done on earth as It is in Heaven, is coming— everyone is awaiting this new era, tired of the present one,** but without knowing what this new thing, this change is about, just as they did not know it when I came upon earth. This expectation is a sure sign that the hour is near. (July 14, 1923)

The several decades that have passed since these words were written down have only caused their truth to grow more obvious. Everyone seems to realize—across religions, nations, cultures, and even in the secular arenas—that the world is on some manner of great cusp. Every day more articles come out wherein the great minds of the world acknowledge that the end of an era is upon us. The imminence of the close of the present age reveals itself in all areas of life: politics, technology, culture, climate science, economics, geological science, finance, and international relations, just to name a few.

Details will not be necessary for most readers, but perhaps a brief presentation of a few is in order for those tempted to pretend all things are "business as usual" or who have a perverse inclination toward a certain alleged habit of ostriches. International relations (especially regarding Russia, China, Iran, North Korea, and Venezuela) seem to indicate World War III is moments away. Scientists are telling us that the world is essentially doomed already due to the wastefulness and exploitation of modern man. The worldwide debt and spending crisis promises an impending implosion that will impoverish billions. All apparent victories against terrorism soon become dwarfed by the new atrocities committed. Earthquakes, wildfires, droughts, blights, and storms are increasing in severity and frequency. In the last several decades alone, the number of children—bonafide, flesh-and-blood, pain-feeling children with literal beating hearts—that have been killed in their own mothers' wombs already far surpasses all the other genocides of history combined. That without which society itself lacks all meaning—the family—is in such utter shambles that the majority of children are now being raised in broken homes. Mass shootings that were in days gone by a once-in-a-decade occurrence at worst are now occurring weekly, if not daily. What technology has become continues to undermine our humanity and promises much more of the same in the days ahead. Suicide has reached historically unprecedented, society-destroying levels, while in Western Nations birthrates have plummeted so low as to have already decimated any humanly possible chance for a flourishing society in the decades to come by distorting the population profile. While some nations drown in food to the point of a never-before-seen obesity epidemic, other nations endure such squalid poverty and famine that millions of children therein continue to die of hunger and easily treatable diseases, while the same companies that own patents on the medicines which could cure them instead pour billions of dollars into developing new cosmetic creams. This list, of course, could be continued for volumes. But, in a word: everyone—except perhaps the most elite of the elite who have leveraged the misery of the masses to their own monetary advantage—is sick and tired of what the world has become. **Everyone knows that "something's got to give." Everyone knows that monumental change is coming.**

But one might protest, "Hold on, these things bode an era of destruction, not of peace!" And indeed, they do bode at least a brief time of necessary—even if unprecedented and universal—convulsions, but as sure as day follows night, the storm is always prelude to clear skies. Deferring again to the wisdom of Tolkien, we know that, "*In the end, the shadow is only a small and passing thing. A new day will dawn, and when the sun shines, it will shine out the clearer.*" No one expects to see his house growing more beautiful by the day even while the old walls are being torn down in order to build the new ones. We will have to wait, however, for the following sections to understand more deeply why, indeed, the Era of Peace really is guaranteed to follow the impending times of distress. For only those who have read the trustworthy prophecies, hitherto known by only a few (a sorry state of affairs I aim to change with this book) have any hope of making sense of the present distress and confusion, and it is only they who have a notion of what comes next. Nevertheless, the universal expectation alone is the sure sign of the coming transformation—and no one can deny that this expectation has reached a veritable fever pitch today.

Now, upon realizing that something is a universal human intuition, only two options exist: one can reject it and thereby smugly assert his own intellectual superiority to almost everyone else in existence, or one can simply recognize that this universal intuition is correct. Even if errors are often mixed in with these intuitions (and indeed they are), the legitimate view of Divine Revelation does not hold that its grace *overrides* nature, but rather that grace *perfects* nature. Thus, this axiom teaches that such intuitions should not be utterly discarded due merely to some errors being mixed in, but instead, teaches that they are to be adjusted and fine-tuned in accord with Divinely revealed truths. Consider the "New Age" movement; although unfortunately containing problematic elements, at least one of its basic intuitions—from which it derives its very name—is spot-on: A New Age of Peace is about to dawn upon the world which will change everything. Even the Vatican itself promulgated a document endorsing the "genuine yearning" in the New Age movement (even while criticizing various errors within it).[1] Far from condemning the fundamental premise that leads many to this movement, the Church praises aspects of it.

But the New Age movement is only one of many realms in which we see the anticipation of the Era. These movements include Christian or quasi-Christian examples: Mormonism, Evangelical Christian Millenarianism, the United Society of Believers in Christ's Second Appearing (Shakers), Jehovah's Witnesses, all of whom are absolutely convinced of the imminent dawn of the Era; as well as non-Christian examples such as Islam's awaiting of the Mahdi, the resurgence of Messianic Judaism, Hindu anticipation of the Mahaparusa, and Buddhist Maitreyan expectation. All of them agree on the fundamental intuition on the coming of the Era. As a professor of philosophy and religion at a public college in New York with students who are Protestants, Catholics, Hindus, Muslims, Sikhs, Buddhists, Zoroastrians, Agnostics, Atheists, and everything in between, I can defer to their testimony; often they have spontaneously shared with me that, in accordance with their own religious or ideological beliefs, they strongly believe that we are now fast approaching the end of an era and the dawn of a new one. Indeed, everyone knows it is coming. Let us, then, look at some of the individuals who have preached it most forcefully; and we can start with those who spoke about it thousands of years ago.

The Fathers of the Church Knew It

Those whom we call Fathers—the great and prolific theologians, saints, doctors, mystics, and philosophers of the early Church, many of whom lived close enough to the time of Christ to still have access to trustworthy and direct oral accounts of His own Divine words, and whom all Christians to this day rightly revere as giving the most authoritative teachings on the Faith—are nearly unanimous in their conviction that earth's final Millennium, which they generally held to be the third after Christ, would host the coming of the Kingdom of God. Here we consider only a tiny fraction of the wealth of their teachings on the matter; with direct quotes from their own writings:

St. Justin Martyr: I and every other orthodox Christian feel certain that there will be a resurrection of the flesh[2] followed by a thousand years in a rebuilt, embellished, and enlarged city of Jerusalem, as was announced by the Prophets Ezekiel, Isaias and others... A man among us named John, one of Christ's Apostles, received and foretold that the followers of Christ would dwell in Jerusalem for a thousand years,[3] and that afterwards the universal and, in short, everlasting resurrection and judgment would take place. (*Dialogue with Trypho.* Ch. 30)

Tertullian: A kingdom is promised to us upon the earth, although before heaven, only in another state of existence; inasmuch as it will be after the resurrection for a thousand years in the divinely-built city of Jerusalem... (*Against Marcion.* Book 3. Ch. 25)

St. Irenaeus: The predicted blessing, therefore, belongs unquestionably to the times of the kingdom... when also the creation, having been renovated and set free, shall fructify with an abundance of all kinds of food, from the dew of heaven, and from the fertility of the earth: as the elders who saw **John, the disciple of the Lord, related that they had heard from** him how the Lord used to teach in regard to these times ... and that all animals feeding [only] on the productions of the earth, should [in those days] become peaceful and harmonious among each other, and be in perfect subjection to man. (*Against Heresies.* Book V. Ch. 33. P. 3)

Lactantius: ...beasts shall not be nourished by blood, nor birds by prey; **but all things shall be peaceful and tranquil. Lions and calves shall stand together at the manger,** the wolf shall not carry off the sheep...These are the things which are spoken of by the prophets as about to happen hereafter: but **I have not considered it necessary to bring forward their testimonies and words, since it would be an endless task**; nor would the limits of my book receive so great a multitude of subjects, since so many with one breath speak similar things; and at the same time, lest weariness should be occasioned to the readers if I should heap together things collected and transferred from all. (*Divine Institutes.* Book 7. Ch. 25)

Having already quoted many sources demonstrating his views on a coming Era of Peace, Lactantius deems it pointless to continue. The task would be so voluminous, he writes— as the same prophecies are given by so many and are thus so clearly undeniable—that its results would be "endless." I, too, conclude this section on the same note, and exhort anyone interested in more details to consult the works of Fr. Joseph Iannuzzi, Mark Mallett, and *The Crown of Sanctity* pages 351-483. While all Christians are duty-bound to believe any unanimous consensus of the Fathers on any matter of Faith (cf. Vatican I, Session 3, §2), the Fathers did have some disagreements on the nature of the Era, so we turn now to another authoritative well-spring of truth: the Magisterium.

The Popes of the Modern Era Have Insisted Upon It

Leading up to—as well as throughout and following—the 20th Century, Papal Magisterium **forcefully proclaimed that the Church was nearing its *Final Confrontation* and the corresponding great triumph to follow.** These Popes insist that the definitive times of Peace not only may come, but *will indeed* come, and that they will not merely constitute *a* peace, but rather *the* very Peace of the Kingdom that Christ came from Heaven to earth to ultimately establish. First, we see the teachings of that great Lion of a Pope, Leo XIII—who, in his famous mystical vision, was shown the reign of Satan during the 20th century (in response to which he instituted the St. Michael the Archangel prayer)—which prophesied times of peace to follow this reign of terror:

> **Pope Leo XIII:** It will at length be possible that our many wounds be healed ... that **the splendors of peace be renewed, and swords and arms drop from the hand when all men shall acknowledge the empire of Christ** and willingly obey His word...(*Annum Sacrum* §11)

To ensure the reader does not assume these words refer merely to the cessation of some specific violent conflict of his day, Leo ends the same paragraph by referring to this very renewal *as the reality described by St. Paul*, when the latter wrote that "Every tongue shall confess that our Lord Jesus Christ is in the glory of God the Father." (Philippians 2:11) But it was Pope St. Pius X, following Leo directly, who truly set the stage for the decades that would follow. On the Feast of St. Francis of Assisi (in whose life we see the beginnings of the restoration of the Order of Eden), in his first Encyclical (explicitly intending to give the figure of his entire pontificate, the very motto of which he declared to be "*To Restore All Things in Christ*") Pius X gave this master plan. Entitled *E Supremi* (On the Restoration of All Things in Christ), it teaches:

> **Pope St. Pius X:** When in every city and village the law of the Lord is faithfully observed ... there will certainly be no more need for us to labor further to see **all things restored in Christ**. Nor is it for the attainment of eternal welfare alone that this will be of service—it will also contribute largely to temporal welfare and the advantage of human society ... when [piety] is strong and flourishing **'the people will' truly 'sit in the fullness of peace'**... May God, "who is rich in mercy", benignly speed **this restoration of the human race in Jesus Christ**... (§14)

Note that he does not teach that all things "might" be restored in Christ, but that they *will* be; not that "some" people will be so restored, but that *the human race* will be. This restoration cannot be anything but a reference to a glorious Era far beyond anything the world has seen since the Fall. We must also place this teaching of Pius X within the context of his insistence, in the same document (§5), that the Antichrist himself was perhaps already in the world; for it is thereby clear that Pius X is insisting that this glorious Era of Peace, which he is here Magisterially prophesying, **is no mere brief period of tranquility** *before* **the cosmic upheavals described in the Book of Revelation, but rather consists in a restoration (on earth and within time) that** *follows* **the defeat of the Antichrist—by a coming,** *in grace,* **of Christ Himself.** This proclamation of a glorious era to come was picked up two decades later by Pius XI—its expectation in no way dimmed by the horror of the First World War—in his proclamation of the Feast of Christ the King, in the Encyclical *Quas Primas*:

> **Pope Pius XI:** When once men recognize, both in private and in public life, that Christ is King, society will at last receive the great blessings of [peace] … If the kingdom of Christ, then, receives, as it should, all nations under its way, **there seems no reason why we should despair of seeing** *that* **peace which the King of Peace came to bring on earth.** (*Quas Primas* §19) [As Jesus taught:] 'And they shall hear my voice, and there shall be one fold and one shepherd.' May God … **bring to fulfillment His prophecy by transforming this consoling vision of the future into a present reality.** (*Ubi Arcano Dei Consilio*)

Now, these prophecies did not end upon the cessation of World War II or upon the fall of the Berlin Wall; as if one could be justified in pretending that such events fulfilled the "peace" spoken of in the prophecies given before their occurrence. Far from it—the same prophecies were still proclaimed by Pope St. John XXIII and Pope St. Paul VI, and more boldly still by Pope St. John Paul II, who, up to his death in 2005, never abandoned his conviction and his teaching that the Third Millennium would see this new glorious Era dawn. In his early days as a Cardinal, he made it clear that the Church was facing its definitive confrontation, but he afterward made it equally clear that the Church would enjoy its splendid triumph following this confrontation:

> **Pope St. John Paul II** (as Cardinal Wojtyla): We are now standing in the face of the greatest historical confrontation humanity has gone through … **We are now facing the final confrontation** between the Church and the anti-Church, of the Gospel versus the anti-Gospel. (*Final speech before departing the U.S.* November 9, 1978) Through your prayers and mine, it is possible to alleviate this tribulation, but it is no longer possible to avert it … the **tears of this century have prepared the ground for a new springtime** of the human spirit. (General Audience. January 24, 2001) **After purification through trial and suffering, the dawn of a new era is about to break.** (General Audience. September 10, 2003)

Although, as we see from his 1978 teaching (one he never retracted or "clarified"), John Paul was convinced that *the* final confrontation was at hand, he was equally convinced that a new springtime would follow. And what was the essence of John Paul's vision of the springtime? *That it would consist in the very Kingdom of God on earth.* For he also taught (and we will revisit this in Chapter 3): "**This is our great hope and our petition: 'Your Kingdom come'—a kingdom of peace, justice, and serenity, that will re-establish the original harmony of creation.**" (General Audience. November 6, 2002) John Paul made it clear that he sees this new Era, to come along with the dawn of the Third Millennium, as a consequence of the "new and Divine" holiness of Living in the Divine Will, which we will speak of later in this same chapter. For, in a formal address to the Rogationist Fathers, he said:

> God himself had provided to bring about that "new and divine" holiness with which the Holy Spirit wishes to enrich Christians at the dawn of the third millennium, in order to "make Christ the heart of the world."

Pope Benedict himself (as Cardinal Ratzinger) confirmed that Pope St. John Paul II saw the Third Millennium as one bound to be a springtime of Christianity and of Christian Reunification. [4] But this teaching of the Popes on the coming Era is no mere remark for the history books: as of my writing these words, it remains the ardent longing of the presently-reigning pontiff; Pope Francis has gone so far as to teach that the prophecies in the Book of Isaiah of universal peace, which some have interpreted as only possibly referring to Heaven, actually refer to a time to be lived *on this earth.*

> **Pope Francis:** Allow me to repeat what the Prophet says; listen carefully: "They shall beat their swords into plowshares, and their spears into pruning hooks; nation shall not lift up sword against nation, neither shall they learn war any more." But when will this occur? **What a beautiful day it shall be, when weapons are dismantled in order to be transformed into tools for work!** What a beautiful day that shall be! And this is possible! Let us bet on hope, on the hope for peace, and it will be possible! (Angelus Address. December 1, 2013)

In a book entitled *Our Father: Reflections on the Lord's Prayer,* published on the fifth anniversary of his elevation to the Papacy, Pope Francis makes clear that this Peace he not only hopes for, but also knows full well *shall* come on earth, is none other than the coming of the Kingdom of God:

> The kingdom of God is here *and* [emphasis in original] the kingdom of God will come. ... the kingdom of God is coming now but at the same time has not yet come completely. This is how the kingdom of God has already come: Jesus has taken flesh... But at the same time there is also the need to cast the anchor there and to hold on to the cord because the Kingdom is still coming...

***

Dear reader, if you are a Catholic who has now completed this section, you know that, in accordance with the promises of Jesus Himself (especially in Matthew 16:18), there exist no grounds on which to doubt the validity of a teaching which is so repeated in the Magisterium of several Popes over the course of more than a century. And if you are a non-Catholic, you are doubtless aware that few if any men on earth rival the Pope of the Roman Church when it comes to knowledge of Scripture, Prophecy, and the Signs of the Times. Consequently, if these men are convicted that a glorious Era of peace is coming... it is quite simply because *a glorious Era of peace is coming.* **We are not left, however, with the words of mere men—holy, learned, and authoritative though they may be—in our sure and certain hope of this coming Era. We also await the Era because Heaven itself has been incessantly pounding the world with revelations (especially during the last 100 years) that promise the Era and implore our efforts to hasten it.**

The Consensus of Prophecy Promises It

Just as an explosion of prophecy preceded the Incarnation itself and grew in fervor and precision the closer the time came to the Word's arrival in the womb of Mary (a dynamic we shall consider more deeply in Chapter 4), so too has the entire world been inundated with Heaven-sent prophecies, particularly in the last century, foretelling the impending close—through great, unprecedented chastisements—of the present sad era, and the following dawn of a new one (equally unprecedented, though in glory). Although such prophecies have existed throughout Church History, we will begin our present consideration with the most famous promise of modern times of the new Era—given at Fatima—and then proceed chronologically, although we will only cover a small fraction of the enormous wealth of trustworthy private revelations that promise the exact same thing. (Note: more details and citations pertaining to the forthcoming prophecies may be found within pages 406-450 of *The Crown of Sanctity*.)

Fatima. Three months before working the most astounding miracle witnessed on earth since Moses lead Israel out of Egypt through the Red Sea (causing, as she did, the sun to dance in the sky before a crowd of 70,000; an event recorded even in the day's secular newspapers), Our Lady promised at Fatima that "The Holy Father will consecrate Russia to me, and she shall be converted, and **an era of peace will be granted to the world.**" But, since a few people attempt to dispute that this sure prophecy refers to a yet to come temporal Era of Peace, let us defer to the teachings of those whose views are worthy of trust on this matter. Cardinal Ciappi was the Theologian of the Pontifical Household to five popes, and Pope St. John Paul II himself gave the cardinal's funeral homily; in it referring to "[Ciappi's] clear thinking, the soundness of his teaching and his undisputed fidelity to the Apostolic See, as well as his *ability to interpret the signs of the times according to God...*"[5] Ciappi, whose view of Fatima should clearly be seen as authoritative, wrote: "…**a miracle was promised at Fatima. And that miracle will be an era of peace, which has never really been granted before to the world...**"[6] Similarly, John Haffert, one of the world's most respected and prolific promoters of the message of Fatima, wrote in *The Great Event*:

> The conversion of the world is sure to come. The world will become His by our conversion and His intervention. .... The Triumph will be a conversion event that will be so powerful and universal that all will be compelled to praise God for the magnificent works He has done in His creature, Mary … **It will be a historical event of such magnitude that it will make all former moments of glory seem like shadows** … (48-49)

In 2016, Monsignor Arthur Calkins, an expert on mystical theology and private revelation, wrote that the triumph of the Immaculate Heart which Our Lady promised at Fatima is *"absolute,"* and "…**will usher in a new era of peace and the spread of Christ's reign, [and] may be much closer than any of us would imagine.**"

Divine Mercy (St. Faustina). St. Faustina, whose revelations have received the highest degree not only of Church approval but of express commendation, wrote in her diary: "In spite of Satan's anger, **The Divine Mercy will triumph over the whole world** and will be worshiped by all souls." (§1789) Here Faustina prophesies a time *on earth* during which there is a triumph of the Faith in all souls alive. For the Last Judgment (the only possible alternative interpretation of this "triumph" about which Faustina speaks) occurs at the definitive end of time and is never referred to as the triumph of *Mercy*; rather, that is always referred to as the time of Universal and Absolute *Justice*. Earlier, Faustina wrote that she prayed for the "triumph of the Church," (§240) and she desired that this triumph be "hastened." (§1581) She would not have written these things if she did not believe such a triumph was possible and willed by God.

Blessed Conchita. Born on the Feast of the Immaculate Conception in the year 1862, and a wife and mother to nine children, Conchita was beatified in May 2019. Among her many prophecies of the Era are the following words of Jesus to her:

> May the whole world have recourse to this Holy Spirit since the day of His reign has arrived. This last stage of the world belongs very specially to Him that He be honored and exalted. May the Church preach Him, may souls love Him, may the whole world be consecrated to

Him, and **peace will come along with a moral and spiritual reaction, greater than the evil by which the world is tormented**... He will come, I will send Him again clearly manifest in His effects, which will astonish the world and impel the Church to holiness...I want to return to the world in My priests. **I want to renew the world** of souls by making Myself seen in My priests.[7]

Servant of God Cora Evans. An American laywoman, mother, and mystic who received revelations from Jesus on the Mystical Humanity of Christ, Cora's cause for Beatification has begun. Jesus told her:

I am giving this gift through you, better to establish My Kingdom of love within souls. I desire all souls to know I am real, alive, and the same today as after My Resurrection. **For My kingdom in souls to be better known is another step in the golden age,** golden because souls in sanctifying grace resemble the light of the golden, noonday sun. In that golden kingdom, I may personally dwell if I am invited... (*Golden Detachment of the Soul*)

Queen of the Universe. In these apparitions which began in 1937 in Heede, Germany—and are not only approved by the Church, but also, according to the Church, enjoy "undeniable proofs of seriousness and authenticity"—the Virgin Mary appeared to four girls with grave messages. Later, in 1945, Jesus appeared to them with His own revelations, exhorting obedience to the earlier messages of His mother, and adding:

I am coming! I am at the door! My love has planned this action before the creation of the world...The world lies in dense darkness. This generation would deserve to be wiped out; but I wish to show Myself merciful...I am coming Myself and I will manifest my will...The things that will come shall surpass by far what happened. The Mother of God, My mother, and the Angels will take part in it. Hell by now believes itself certain of victory, but I will take it away...**I am coming, and with me peace shall come. I will build my Kingdom** with a small number of elect. This Kingdom will come suddenly, sooner than what one thinks. I will make My light shine, which to some will be blessing and to others darkness. Humanity will recognize my love and my power.

Our Lady of America. This well-known Marian apparition has many associated Church approvals (including approbation from Archbishop Leibold and a strong endorsement by Cardinal Raymond Burke) and consists in visitations from the Blessed Virgin to a religious, Sister Mary Ephrem (also often referred to by her baptismal name, Mildred Mary Neuzil), in Indiana in the year 1956. She was told:

There will remain a remnant untouched by the chaos who, having been faithful in following Me and spreading My warnings, will gradually inhabit the earth again with their dedicated and holy lives. These souls will renew the earth in the power and light of the Holy Spirit, and these faithful children of Mine will be under My protection, and that of the Holy Angels, **and they will partake of the life of the Divine Trinity in a most remarkable way**...

Lady of All Nations (Ida Peerdeman). In these approved apparitions to Ida Peerdeman, a woman living in Amsterdam, Netherlands, in the mid-20th century, Our Lady gave many prophecies that have already been fulfilled with startling accuracy (whoever wishes to learn more about them should read Dr. Mark Miravalle's exposition on these incredible events). In the messages, we see the following:

When the dogma, the last dogma of the Marian mystery, will have been promulgated, it will be then that the Lady of All Peoples will give peace to the world, true peace ... [The Lady] comes to announce the Holy Spirit. The Holy Spirit will then come over this earth.

Venerable Marthe Robin. A French mystic and stigmatist who died in 1981, Venerable

Marthe's cause for beatification began only six years after her death, and in 2014 her heroic virtues were formally recognized by the Vatican, thus honoring her with the title *Venerable*. Regarding her revelations, Hugh Owen writes:

> On September 29, 1930, Marthe had prayed for "the mighty hour of the harvest, when Good will triumph, when faith will flourish everywhere, and when the living flame of love will be ignited in all hearts." Keeping in mind that "the living flame of love" refers unmistakably to the Holy Spirit, can Marthe have been foretelling anything less revolutionary than the Triumph of the Immaculate Heart and the Reign of the Holy Spirit in the world? Indeed, according to Fr. Finet, Marthe had predicted in 1936 that "there would be a New Pentecost of Love, that the Church would be renewed by an apostolate of the laity."

Fr. Ottavio Michelini. A priest, mystic, and member of the Papal Court of Pope St. Paul VI (one of the highest honors bestowed by a Pope on a living person), Fr. Ottavio received many revelations, documented in the 1976 book entitled *Thou Knowest That I Love Thee*. In this book, we read:

> It will be the Mother, **most holy Mary, who will crush the head of the serpent, thus beginning a new era of peace; it will be the advent of my Kingdom upon earth.** It will be the return of the Holy Ghost for a new Pentecost. Hell will be defeated: my Church will be regenerated: My Kingdom, that is a kingdom of love, of justice and of peace, will give peace and justice to this humanity. (December 10, 1976) [The earth] will be made arid and desolate then "purified" by fire to be fertilized by the honest labor of the just escaped for the divine goodness to the tremendous hour of the divine anger. [Then] **there will be the reign of God in the souls, that reign the just ask from God invoking "Thy Kingdom come."** (January 2, 1979)

Sr. Natalia of Hungary. A 20th-century nun whose messages bear a *nihil obstat* and an *imprimatur*, Sr. Natalia was given revelations from Jesus and Mary which read:

> The end of sin is close, but not the end of the world. Soon no more souls will be lost. My words will be fulfilled, and there will only be one flock and one Shepherd. (Jn. 10:16) Pray, so that before the holy peace, and the great mercy for the world arrives, sinners may be converted and accept my mercy, amending their lives. . . . [The Virgin Mary revealed:] The age of world peace is not delayed. The Heavenly Father only wants to give time to those who are able to be converted and find refuge with God. . ." The Savior showed me that unceasing love, happiness and divine joy will signify [the] future clean world. I saw the blessing of God abundantly poured out upon the earth. Jesus then explained to me: ". . .the arrival of the era of paradise, when mankind will live as without sin. There will be a new world and a new era. It will be the era when humanity will recover what it lost in paradise. When my Immaculate Mother steps on the neck of the serpent..."

Elizabeth Kindelmann. The "flame of love" revelations to Elizabeth Kindelmann, a 20th-century Hungarian wife and mother, were approved by no fewer than four Archbishops (including two Cardinals and Archbishop Chaput). In them, we read:

> [After being shown a vision, Elizabeth wrote:] my heart overflowed with a huge cheerfulness . . . I saw how Satan becomes blinded, and also the beneficial effects that men will reap from it, in the whole world. Under the effect of that gladness, I could hardly close my eyes during the whole night, and when a light sleep came on me, my guardian angel woke me saying: "How can you sleep like that, with such a great gladness which will shake the world?" [Immediately after her guardian angel said these words, Jesus revealed to Elizabeth more about what this blinding of Satan entails. Jesus said:] That Satan becomes blind means the world triumph of my Sacred-Heart, the liberation of souls, and that the road of Salvation will open in all its plenitude. (November 13th-14th, 1964) [In an undated entry from August 1962, Jesus said to

Elizabeth:] **Let the coming of my Kingdom be the aim of your life on earth.**

Alicja Lenczewska. A Polish mystic and saintly woman who died in 2001 and received revelations from Jesus, Alicja had her messages approved in 2017. Below is a small selection of her messages from Jesus which prophesy a Glorious Era of Peace:

> Satan and his servants will rejoice—as they rejoiced then in Jerusalem. But the time of their apparent victory will be short, for the morning will come of the Resurrection of the Holy Church, immortal, giving birth to new life on earth—the holiness of My children. (November 11, 2000) The Immaculate Heart of My Mother will triumph...the dawn and spring of the Holy Church is coming...A purification will be given that will bring the sons of darkness to the light of God's Truth, and every person will according to their own will in the light of that Truth have to choose the Kingdom of My Father or give themselves over eternally to the father of lies ... **Mary is the one through whom will come the rebirth of My Church, so that it would shine with the full splendor of God's Holiness.** (June 8, 2002)

Servant of God Maria Esperanza. Maria Esperanza was a wife, mother, mystic, and recipient of the apparitions at Betania, Venezuela (approved by the Bishop in 1987). She died in 2004, and her cause for beatification has already officially opened. Michael Brown, a Catholic journalist who often spoke to her and knew her personally, wrote the following of her prophecies: "It was Esperanza's view that Jesus would soon come in a different way than He did 2,000 years ago ... what she called an 'awakening' ... and that He would come 'in the same way as He resurrected, as an apparition. That's why I have been saying to be ready, because things are starting to happen...'" In his book, *Call of the Ages*, Dr. Petrisko shares more of Esperanza's teachings regarding the Era:

> In many interviews, Maria has spoken of the coming times. She indicates somewhat that she knows what the Era of Peace may be like and what it may bring... "The environment will be fresh and new, and we will be happy in our world, without the feeling of tension...This century is purifying; after will come peace and love...It will be in a way never before imagined by man, because the Light of His New Rising will be evident to everyone. And of course, man is still not ready for this, to accept these profound things, which actually are so simple and so clear, just as the water which comes down from the spring." ... [The Lord told Esparanza:] "I will come among you in a resplendent sun. My rays will reach all nations to illuminate you, to enlighten you, that you may rise and grow as plants grow, with fruits. You all have the right to receive the grace of God the Father." (469-470)

Apostolate of Holy Motherhood. An anonymous young mother ("Mariamante") received messages from Jesus and Mary in 1987 and these locutions are compiled in a book entitled *The Apostolate of Holy Motherhood*, which received both a *nihil obstat* and an *imprimatur*. Compiled and edited by Dr. Mark Miravalle, it reads:

> This Era of Peace which will encompass the world will be the result of the Triumph of the Immaculate Heart of Mary, My Mother. **The deplorable conditions in which the world now finds itself will be transformed into the likeness of My Father's Kingdom** for a time, and there will be peace. I say again, rejoice that you are privileged to live in this era. ...The salvation of many souls is at stake. This is why so many extraordinary graces are being poured forth. The Era of My Mercy has come. It will **unite Heaven and earth in one hymn of love to the Blessed Trinity.** I call you to rejoicing. The time has come. So be it. Amen.

Barnabas Nwoye (Precious Blood Revelations). A Nigerian man who has been receiving messages from Heaven centering on the Precious Blood of Jesus since childhood, Barnabas' prayer book associated with his revelations, *Precious Blood of Jesus Daily*

Devotional, was given a *nihil obstat*, and in it we read the following revealed prayers:

> Agonizing Jesus, I offer You my heart to be united with Your Agonizing Heart as a co-bearer of Your agony. Jesus, I wish to be in agony with You so as to hasten Your Glorious Reign of Peace. Amen. Eternal Father, You are the creator and author of life. You love the world You made. That is why **You sent Your only-begotten Son to come for its redemption, so that Your Kingdom will come.** ... I offer You all the sufferings, pains, and death of Your only begotten Son Whom You love, **for Your triumph and reign on earth**.

Fr. Stefano Gobbi (Marian Movement of Priests). The founder of the Marian Movement of Priests, Fr. Gobbi, was an Italian priest, mystic, and theologian who died in 2011 and was the recipient of revelations (locutions) recorded in "the Blue Book," the actual title of which is, *To the Priests, Our Lady's Beloved Sons*. This book bears full Ecclesiastical approbation; having an *imprimatur* from Bishops and Cardinals who not only approved these revelations, but also strongly encouraged their promotion. In them, we read multitudes of prophecies regarding the Era, a small selection of which are as follows:

> Jesus, Who taught you the prayer for asking for the coming of God's kingdom upon earth, will at last see this prayer of His fulfilled, for He will establish His Kingdom. And creation will return to being a new garden in which Christ will be glorified by all and His divine Kingship will be welcomed and exalted; it will be a universal Kingdom of Grace, beauty, harmony, communion, justice and peace. (July 3, 1987) In the hour of the great trial, *paradise will be joined to earth,* until the moment when the luminous door will be opened, to cause to descend upon the world the glorious presence of Christ, who will restore his reign in which the divine Will shall be accomplished in a perfect manner, as in heaven, so also on earth. (November 1, 1990) *The new era,* which I announce to you, coincides with the complete fulfillment of the divine will, so that at last there is coming about that which Jesus taught you to ask for, from the Heavenly Father: 'Your will be done on earth as it is in heaven.' This is the time when the divine will of the Father, of the Son and of the Holy Spirit is being accomplished by the creatures. From the perfect fulfillment of the divine will, the whole world is becoming renewed. (August 15, 1991)

Our Lady of Zaro. The apparitions of Our Lady of Zaro began in 1994 to several members of a prayer group in the diocese of Ischia in Southern Italy, and within Our Lady's messages here we read:

> At one point, I saw something like a great sun illuminating the whole *earth* and Mother told me: "Behold, **when my heart will triumph everything will shine more than the sun.**" (December 26, 2018) ... everything stops: evil disappears, the screams and pain, the dead are gone, **a great peace reigns and a single prayer is heard rising to heaven... My beloved children, learn to say to the Lord "Thy Will be done" and learn to accept it.** (August 8, 2018) Go forward with courage and with the weapon of the Holy Rosary in your hands, pray for the salvation of souls and for the conversion of all humanity. Hard times await you, but do not turn away, be perseverant, because with your prayer and your suffering you can save many souls. My children, your ears will hear distant noises and clashes of war, the earth will yet tremble, but I am with you, do not be afraid; **after the tribulation there will be peace and my Immaculate heart will triumph.** (May 8, 2018)

Gladys Quiroga (San Nicolas). Under the title of Our Lady of the Rosary, the Virgin Mary has appeared to Gladys Quiroga de Motta, a wife and mother, since 1983. In 2016, many of the apparitions (those received up to 1990) were officially declared to be "of supernatural origin" and worthy of belief by the Church. World-renowned theologian Fr. Rene Laurentin both promoted and wrote extensively on these apparitions, and hundreds of thousands of pilgrims have visited the apparition site. Our Lady revealed to Gladys:

If [man] desired to discover God, this would be an earth of peace for all, because only God can make peace reign, that peace so longed for by many! (June 7, 1985) The Holy Church will soon come to shine like the brightest of stars. Glory be to God. Make it known. (November 9, 1986) **The most intense Light of Christ will rise again. As at the Calvary, after the Crucifixion and death came the Resurrection, the Church will also be reborn by the strength of Love.** ...You must make this known! (July 10, 1988)

In Sinu Jesu. The book, *In Sinu Jesu: When Heart Speaks to Heart—The Journal of a Priest at Prayer*, contains the locutions received by an anonymous Benedictine monk beginning in the year 2007, and is considered authentic by the monk's spiritual director. It contains both an *imprimatur* and a *nihil obstat* and is strongly endorsed by Cardinal Raymond Burke and many others. In it, Jesus tells this priest-monk:

My Immaculate Mother will instruct [priests] and, by her all-powerful intercession, obtain for them all the charisms necessary to prepare the world—this sleeping world—for My return in glory. I tell you this not to alarm you or to frighten anyone, but to give you cause for an immense hope and for pure spiritual joy. The renewal of My priests will be the beginning of the renewal of My Church ...**I will undo the destruction [the demons] have wrought and I will cause My priests and My Spouse the Church to recover a glorious holiness that will confound My enemies and be the beginning of a new era of saints.** (March 2, 2010) The day is coming, and it is not far off ... when I will intervene to triumph in My Eucharistic Heart by the conquering power of sacrificial love alone; when I will intervene to defend the poor and vindicate the innocents whose blood has marked this nation and so many others as did the blood of Abel in the beginning. (November 12, 2008) If more souls would give Me this freedom to act as I will, My Church would begin to know the springtime of holiness that is My burning desire for her. **These souls, by their entire submission to all the dispositions of My providence, will be the ones to usher in My kingdom of peace and holiness on earth.**

Edson Glauber (Itapiranga, Brazil). In 2010, Bishop Carillo Gritti approved a series of decades-long apparitions to a Brazilian man, Edson, declaring them to be of supernatural origin.[8] Dr. Mark Miravalle, the world-renowned theologian and Mariologist, wrote an entire book on them entitled *The Three Hearts*. This book relays the results of his investigation into the apparitions, for which he even traveled to South America and extensively interviewed Edson, who received the following messages from Heaven:

The Lord is returning to fulfil all his promises. His kingdom on earth will be as it is in Heaven. (July 8, 2000) Strive for the kingdom of heaven; not long remains before your and the world's definitive liberation from all evil. God is sending me, your Most Holy Mother, in order to prepare you for the great final battle against all evil ... You are already in the times of the great transformations of the world and the Lord God is already marking his chosen ones, those who are obedient to Heaven's voice. (September 29, 2003) I desire [to have] saints for my kingdom of love. **The earth will yet be a great paradise.** First will come the sorrows, but then will come the great transformation, when all will be renewed and all things will be made new. Humanity will be revived in love and peace. Thus my kingdom on earth will be as in heaven. (March 23, 2004) There will be no more suffering. There will be no more weeping. God will wipe away the tears of all those who hope with patience and do not lose faith. Little children, take heart. Courage. A while more and everything will be transformed. (August 7, 2005)

Pedro Regis. A seer from Anguera, Brazil, Pedro has been receiving messages for decades and enjoys the support of his Bishop, who stated: "I have already reached the conclusion that, from the pastoral point of view, the meeting in Angüera [Pedro's revelations] is valid." Pedro was told by Jesus and Mary:

I want to make you saints for the glory of the reign of God. Open your hearts! **Very soon the world will be transformed into a new world, without hate or violence. The world will be a new garden** and all will live happily. (October 8, 1988) I want you to be a part of the Lord's victorious army. The Lord has reserved a great Grace for His own. He will transform humanity into a new garden. **When all this happens the world will abound with goods and man will lack nothing.** It will be a time when the fruits of trees will be multiplied and there will be two crops per year. Hunger will no longer exist for humanity. (June 3, 2000) Whatever happens, stay with Jesus. He is in control of everything. Trust in Him and you will see the transformation of the earth. **Humanity will be made new by the Mercy of Jesus.** A great sign from God will appear, and mankind will be astonished. Those separated will be led to the truth and great faith will possess the elect of the Lord. (December 24, 2011) Those who remain faithful until the end will be called blessed by the Father. Do not allow the flame of faith to be extinguished within you. You still have long years of trials ahead of you, but the great day is coming. My Jesus will give you the grace to live in complete peace. The Earth will be completely transformed **and all will live joyfully.** (December 24, 2013)

Queen of Peace (Medjugorje). The apparitions at Medjugorje, while neither approved nor condemned, have recently seen many positive developments in the Church and have become among the most famous and abundantly fruitful Marian Apparitions in history. One of the seers, Mirjana, recently published a book, the very title of which speaks of the Era of Peace. Entitled *My Heart Will Triumph*, we see in it the following:

Our Lady is planning to change the world. She did not come to announce our destruction; she came to save us, and with her Son, **she will triumph over evil.** If our Mother has promised to defeat evil, then what do we have to fear? (Chapter 14) [Our Lady] asked for our prayers, **"so that as soon as possible a time of peace, for which my heart waits impatiently, may reign."** (Chapter 26) After the events take place as predicted, it will be difficult for even the staunchest skeptics to doubt the existence of God. (Chapter 13) Some seem to think that all the secrets are negative. Maybe they have a guilty conscience; maybe they are afraid of how they've lived their life and so they fear God's punishment. Perhaps when we do not have enough good inside, we expect bad things. ... The people who are concerned about the secrets have not seen Our Lady and do not know about God's complete project—why Our Lady comes here at all, or what she's preparing us for. (Chapter 14)

Luz de Maria. This Argentinian laywoman and mother of eight children (one of whom is a priest) began receiving messages from Heaven in the 1990s, and still receives revelations that speak explicitly about Living in the Divine Will and its impending Universal Reign on earth in a Glorious Era of Peace. Her revelations, in fact, are so significant that she was granted a meeting with Pope St. John Paul II three separate times, and twice with Pope Benedict XVI. Her bishop not only approved her messages and gave them the Church's *imprimatur*, but strongly advocated for them, writing, "These Messages are an explanation from Heaven in these moments in which man must remain attentive to not go astray from the Divine Word. ... I ask the Virgin Mary, Mother of God and Our Mother, to intercede for us so that the Will of God be fulfilled '...on earth as it is in Heaven.'" These revelations include the following prophecies:

[An] Era [is coming] in which everything will be reborn; man, purified and fused with God's Will, Creation, which will then feel in harmony with mankind. Total and complete happiness. Peace and harmony are coming. (January 30, 2011) The new dawn will come for My children. Evil will not find a place among men and all will be peace. My children will see in all of

Creation the seed of My Love. My Mother will camp with Her children; the lost gifts will be deserved by man again and I will see Myself pleased in each human being. All of the Cosmos will vibrate with the beating of My Heart to a single unique rhythm, and man will breathe My Peace in total concordance. (February 26, 2011) **In the end, the Immaculate Heart of my mother will triumph, and my Divine Will, will reign on earth as … in Heaven.** (July 7, 2014)

※※※

Limitations of space demand that I leave untouched the vast majority of revelations which prophesy the Era. But from the small sample considered here, we already see an overwhelming consensus in private revelation as to the guaranteed coming of this Glorious Age, to be lived on earth before the end of time. Any dismissal of the Era, therefore, is none other than a blanket dismissal of private revelation, thus implying that the *sensus fidelium* (sense of the faithful) can err (a notion which, in turn, is condemned by the Catechism (§492) and *Lumen Gentium* (§12)) by an entire century of prophets—trustworthy, saintly souls, across the entire world—being systematically and radically deceived on one of their fundamental and unanimous tenets.

This limitation also restricted our focus to 20th-century private revelation—as this century stood on the cusp of the Era, Heaven spoke about the Era more clearly during its years than in the centuries prior. But the Era was by no means unheard of in those earlier private revelations. On the contrary, **prophecies that promise the Era have been given abundantly throughout the entire history of the Church.** Already in 1914, the old Catholic Encyclopedia, of unassailable orthodoxy and great authority, makes this clear in its article on *Prophecy*, which sums up the main thrust and overarching themes of 1,900 years of private revelation:

> The more noteworthy of the prophecies bearing upon "latter times" seem to have **one common end**, to announce great calamities impending over mankind, **the triumph of the Church, and the renovation of the world.** *All the seers agree* … they *all* promise for the Church a victory more splendid than she has *ever* achieved here below.

Indeed, up until very recently—when a few noisy men who have published their own Era-free eschatological speculations decided to make condemning the Era their whole mission—this fact was always taken for granted. Consider, for example, the work of Fr. Charles Arminjon, in his series of retreats at the Cathedral of Chambéry in the 18th century, which, collected into articles, has only recently been translated into English and published under the title *The End of the Present World and the Mysteries of the Future Life.* St. Thérèse of Lisieux said of this book, "This reading was one of the greatest graces of my life… the impressions I received are too deep to express in human words." Among many other eschatological teachings within it, Fr. Arminjon presents the following:

> The most authoritative view, and the one that appears to be most in harmony with Holy Scripture, is that, after the fall of the Antichrist, the Catholic Church will once again enter upon a period of prosperity and triumph … These words are formal, and appear to leave no room for doubt. (Page 57)

Here, Fr. Arminjon is simply confirming what the great minds before him (e.g. St. Louis de Montfort, St. John Vianney, Venerable Mary of Agreda, St. John Bosco, and many others) taught regarding the reality of the coming Era of Peace: it will be glorious, it will be on earth, and there is *no* room for doubting its arrival.

Despite all this, those who believe in the Era can still plan on occasionally hearing repeated the old denunciation, "forget your utopian delusions of grandeur!" For those words seem to always lie in wait upon the lips of the jaded cynics who haunt the pews of some Churches; with these and similar pronouncements they lecture those who harbor hope for a new Era, ready as they always are to pounce upon the least suggestion that the world need not always be as it is now. Such cynics should be reminded that belief in God is a dangerous thing. For this belief entails a recognition that the course of history shall be left neither to chance, nor to the machinations of man, nor the uninterrupted perpetuation of trends that have only for a passing time been observed (even if that duration of time, in the eyes of those who are fixated upon the temporal, seems so long as to be identifiable with eternity itself). We have seen, from all the preceding sections, *that such cynicism is nothing but a Dystopian Delusion of Insipidness.* The Era is coming, friends. No one can stop it.

Does anyone now, having read the preceding pages, doubt its arrival? I hope not. But we still have not arrived at the clearest proof yet—for many of the prophetic sources already considered give only small sips of the glory of the Era to their readers. *What we will consider next gives torrents.*

It Has Been Foretold by an Absolutely Trustworthy Source

Several decades ago, an ordinary Italian woman named Luisa Piccarreta wrote thousands of pages of messages from Jesus Himself; messages pertaining to a certain Gift—the Gift of Living in the Divine Will—and heralding the imminent universal Reign of the glory of this Gift. Though Luisa's humility was such that she wanted only to be unknown, poor, chaste, obedient, and forgotten (among her greatest sufferings was her embarrassment that the Church insisted upon publishing her volumes)—she was nevertheless directly commanded by God (and by Ecclesiastical authorities of the Church) to write down everything Jesus told her so that, when the time was ripe, these astounding revelations that permeate her writings could bear their intended fruit throughout the entire world by ushering in the Reign of the Divine Will on earth as in Heaven in fulfillment of the Our Father prayer itself. *That time has finally arrived.* Although all the revelations, the Fathers, the Popes, etc., we discussed in the previous sections speak of this Era, only Luisa's revelations are *fully* capable of relaying the *essence* of the Era and thereby most powerfully hastening its Reign; for the Era's essence is none other than the very Gift of which her revelations speak.

We must first, however, settle beyond doubt why we know these revelations to Luisa are true, and only thereafter shall we consider more of their content (note: more details and citations may be found in *The Crown of Sanctity*, pages 69-86).

During Luisa's life:

- **Miraculously, Luisa lived most of her 81-year long life with only the Eucharist for food.** From age 22 onward, she was bedridden, but never suffered a diagnosed illness (and never even was afflicted with a single bedsore). Each morning her body was rendered rigid as rock; she was incapable of moving, and (mysteriously) no one else—no matter how strong—was physically capable of moving her; that is, until a priest came in to bless her each morning, at which point she was miraculously and instantaneously relieved from this state. Doctor after doctor and expert after expert examined her and none could explain the phenomena.[9] All these facts have always been known by all who honestly investigated them, but in 2016 they were confirmed by the Vatican's own official biography of Luisa, *The Sun of My Will* (see Chapters IV and VIII). Indeed, no life has ever been as lowly—as utterly dependent upon God and upon the Church—as Luisa's. But how could it fail to be so that the soul entrusted with so superlative a mission be herself so very lowly? (cf. Luke 1:48)

- **St. Hannibal di Francia became the most zealous of all promoters of Luisa's revelations.** He was appointed by the Bishop to be Luisa's spiritual director, and became so convicted of the validity and urgency of her revelations that he dedicated the last decades of his life to promulgating them, writing (just four months before his death), *"I have totally dedicated myself to the great work of the Divine Will, I practically don't concern myself at all with my institutes."*[10] He wrote that Luisa's revelations consist in**"... a mission so sublime that no other can be compared to it—that is, the triumph of the Divine Will upon the whole earth, in conformity with what is said in the 'Our Father.'"** In the Vatican's official biography of Luisa, we read that Hannibal said her writings **"must be made known to the world."** (117) Also within this authoritative volume's pages, we see that Hannibal said that Luisa "... never, for any reason in the world, would have put into writing her intimate and prolonged communications with revered Jesus ... if Our Lord himself had not repeatedly obliged her to do so, both personally and through holy obedience to her directors ... [This] purest virgin, wholly of God ... emerges to be a singular predilection of the Divine Redeemer, Jesus Our Lord, who century after century, increases ever more the wonders of His love. It seems that He wanted to form this virgin, whom He calls the littlest one He found on earth, and bereft of any education, into an instrument of a mission so sublime, that is, the triumph of the Divine Will..." (122-123)
- **St. Hannibal gave 19 of Luisa's works his own** *nihil obstat.* (cf. *New Catholic Encyclopedia.* 2nd Edition. Volume 5. Page 866.)
- **Archbishop Joseph Leo gave his** *imprimaturs* **to 20 sets of Luisa's revelations.**
- **Pope St. Pius X himself believed Luisa's** *Hours of the Passion* **were thoroughly authentic,** saying to St. Hannibal (who was friends with the Pope), after he read an excerpt from them: *"Father, this book should be read while kneeling: it is Jesus Christ who is speaking!"*[11]
- **St. Padre Pio strongly endorsed Luisa** and was even known to say to pilgrims who came to him from Corato to go see Luisa instead. The aforementioned official, Church-sanctioned biography of Luisa dedicates a section to the relationship between Luisa and Padre Pio and confirms its authenticity, even asserting that Padre Pio affirmed Luisa worked a miracle, as he said, "Yes, by the intercession of Luisa Piccarreta, the Lord has saved [a dying girl]." (174-175)
- **Luisa's death was itself miraculous and her funeral was one only a saint's life could have generated.** Regarding these events, we again read in the Vatican's official biography all the following facts (quoted verbatim where noted). Her body "never developed rigor mortis" and her "eyes could be seen bright as before without the film of death." An entire group of doctors had to be called in just to confirm she was "really dead," a study which itself took four days, during which "no sign of corruption,"—that is, the ordinary decay that all bodies begin undergoing immediately after death and is easily detectable

mere hours later—could be observed anywhere in her body (and nor was there any odor). Despite the lack of rigor mortis, one thing absolutely could not be moved: her upper torso, which insisted upon remaining in the upright position it had assumed while Luisa was writing down Jesus' revelations to her. After many failed attempts to lay her body flat, the funeral workers gave up and instead had a special casket built which allowed her body to remain in this position. Crowds upon crowds poured in to pay homage to the body of "Luisa the Saint" (what she was known as during her life), and to witness these amazing phenomena firsthand. The funeral was a "holiday for all Corato" with even newspapers covering the event, a day "etched in people's minds as something extraordinary." Almost immediately, news of this reached—of all places— Brooklyn, New York, where devotion to Luisa was thus initiated. Three weeks after Luisa's death, her confessor wrote a letter to a certain "Tommasino," who lived there, and this letter was promptly published in a newspaper on April 13th. It reads in part: "I was with [Luisa] up until the last moment… she died like the saints die…I am still recovering from the tremendous shock…Her funeral? … A real triumph! … A truly rare sight, perhaps unparalleled, and whoever had the good fortune to take part will never be able to—and never know how—to express how magnificent it was…" (*The Sun of My Will*, 179-187)

Since Luisa's Death:

- November 20th, 1994: Cardinal Joseph Ratzinger nullifies the previous condemnations of Luisa's writings, allowing Luisa's cause to formally open on the Feast of Christ the King of the same year.

- February 2nd, 1996: Pope St. John Paul II permits the copying of Luisa's original volumes, which up until then had been reserved in the Vatican Archives.

- October 7th, 1997: Pope St. John Paul II beatifies Hannibal Di Francia after expressly making his own St. Hannibal's belief in 1)The Universality, 2) The Prophetic Nature, and 3) The New Holiness of Luisa's revelations, saying **"[St. Hannibal saw] the means God himself had provided to bring about that 'new and divine' holiness with which the Holy Spirit wishes to enrich Christians at the dawn of the third millennium, in order to 'make Christ the heart of the world.'"**[12]

- June 2nd & December 18th, 1997: **The two Church-appointed theologians submit their evaluations of Luisa's writings to the Diocesan tribunal, affirming that *nothing* in them is contrary to Catholic Faith or Morals.**

- **May 16th, 2004: Pope St. John Paul II canonizes Hannibal Di Francia.**

- October 29th, 2005, the diocesan tribunal and the Archbishop of Trani, Giovanni Battista Pichierri, render a positive judgment on Luisa after carefully examining all of her writings and testimony on her heroic virtue; rendering her status as "Servant of God" no mere procedural step, but a veritable Ecclesiastical Approbation of her holiness and authenticity.

- July 24th, 2010, both Theological Censors (whose identities are secret) appointed by the Holy See give their approval to Luisa's writings, promulgating yet another assertion that nothing contained within them is opposed to Faith or Morals.

- **April 12th, 2011, Bishop Luigi Negri approves the Benedictine Daughters of the Divine Will, a religious order explicitly dedicated to Luisa's Divine Will spirituality, founded** by a holy nun from Mother Angelica's order.

- November 22nd, 2012, the faculty of the Pontifical Gregorian University in Rome who reviewed Fr. Joseph Iannuzzi's Doctoral Dissertation defending and explaining Luisa's revelations give it unanimous approval, thereby granting its contents ecclesiastical approval authorized by the Holy See. In the following two years, this Dissertation received the accolades of almost fifty[13] Catholic Bishops.

- 2014: Fr. Edward O'Connor, theologian and long-time professor of theology at Notre Dame University, publishes his last book, *Living in the Divine Will: the Grace of Luisa Piccarreta*, strongly endorsing her revelations.

- April, 2015: Maria Margarita Chavez reveals that she was miraculously healed through the intercession of Luisa eight years earlier; followed by an official Diocesan investigation.[14]

- January, 2016: *The Sun of My Will*, the official biography of Luisa Piccarreta quoted earlier, is **published by the Vatican's own official publishing house**. Authored by Maria Rosario Del Genio, it **contains a preface by Cardinal Jose Saraiva Martins, Prefect Emeritus of the Congregation for the Causes of Saints, strongly endorsing Luisa *and* her revelations from Jesus. In this preface, he states that the "Living in the Divine Will"** revealed to Luisa *is in fact* "**the actual way in which the Son Jesus lived on earth, bringing here with him the life of heaven.**" (Considering the Cardinal's position, if anyone alive knows what makes a saint and an authentic revelation, it is he who does!) The same year, the Vatican publishes its own authoritative Dictionary of Mysticism, in which Luisa is given her own entry (page 1266).

- November, 2018: Another official Diocesan inquiry into a miraculous healing through Luisa is initiated, this time of a man named Laudir Floriano Waloski in Brazil, and around this time the Vatican grants permission for Luisa's body to be moved to the center of the Church in which it had hitherto occupied only a less-emphasized location.

For one who acknowledges the proper means of discerning any alleged revelation, mystic, or seer, there is no longer any doubt. Nowhere in the entire history of the Church will one find a mystic whose cause has seen a similar degree of success as Luisa's, whose life was as fruitful as Luisa's and exhibited the endorsements that Luisa's did, and whose legacy remained totally unmarred even for decades after death—but who later proved to be a fraud or an agent of the devil. **Indeed, this lowly Italian woman, Luisa Piccarreta, experienced mystical phenomena and endured sacrifices of such magnitude that they are not rivaled anywhere, anytime. These phenomena existed for a reason: because the soul experiencing them is also going to be entrusted with revelations. These revelations call for our response and are of such a magnitude that the likes of these, too, have been seen nowhere in history.** This changes everything. And there simply is no turning back.

I did leave out something rather important from the timeline above, however: Luisa's condemnation. Three of her works were placed on the Index of Prohibited Books, and this placement was promulgated on September 11th, 1938. A mere month after these works were placed on the index, the superiors reacted by expelling her from the convent in which she had been living for a decade. This condemnation of her works (which is today in no way, shape, or form binding) was an important element of the Divine Plan, so that Luisa could be more perfectly conformed to the image of Jesus Christ, who also was condemned by the legitimate Ecclesiastical authority of His day. And we see a similar dynamic in many of the most important saints and mystics of the Church—Padre Pio, St. Teresa of Avila, St. Joan of Arc—but especially St. Faustina, whose revelations sat on the same Index alongside Luisa's.[15] When news of the condemnation reached Luisa, Jesus told her:

> Unite in My Will Our condemnation to the one I received when I was Crucified and I will give you the merit of My condemnation and all the Goods that It produces: It made me die, then It called to Life My Resurrection … I will make My Truths rise again more beautifully-more majestic, in the midst of the peoples… My daughter, what is not enjoyed today, will be enjoyed tomorrow; what now seems darkness because it finds blind minds, will turn into sun tomorrow for those who have eyes. How much Good they will do. (September 18, 1938)

Two months after her expulsion from the convent, Luisa finished her last writing, as she was no longer bound to write upon its completion—and she put down the pen as obediently as she had picked it up forty years earlier. One year later, World War II began. Nine years later, on March 4th, 1947, she breathed her last.

> My daughter, the Will of God that the Writings of My Divine Will come to light is absolute, and as many incidents as may occur, It will triumph of everything. And even if it should take years and years, It will know how to dispose everything so that Its absolute Will be fulfilled. The time in which they will come to light is relative and conditional upon when creatures dispose themselves to receive a good so great, and upon those who must occupy themselves with being its criers, and make the sacrifice so as to bring the new era of peace, the new Sun that will dispel all the clouds of evils. (Jesus to Luisa. August 2, 1928)

Fifty-eight years later, all condemnations nullified, her cause for beatification and canonization proceeded triumphantly to the Vatican itself.

Luisa's Prophecies Fulfilled

Imagine set before you a stack of pages relating certain events—pages which you know, with documented proof to bolster your certainty, were written long before the events themselves. Imagine that these pages specifically foretell World War II, some of modern history's most devastating earthquakes, some of the 20th century's most significant events, Globalization, the abuse crisis in the Church, the canonization of a saint, and much more. You would, no doubt, be utterly awed and would not question for a moment that their author was truly a prophet who received messages from Heaven.

Well, this is no figment of anyone's imagination; this is, rather, exactly what we in fact have with Luisa's revelations, which seem to have **more fulfilled prophecies within their pages than any other private revelation**. Dare to doubt if you will, but all the following prophecies can be easily authenticated with your own research. Furthermore, what I present here are just a few fulfilled prophecies that I recall from my own reading of Luisa's writings. Dive into the writings yourself, and I am sure you will discover many more. As St. Hannibal (who died long before Luisa stopped writing) himself said, regarding Luisa's writings:

> There are chapters which foresee divine scourges of earthquakes, wars, fire, cloudbursts, devastation of lands, epidemics, famines and the like. **Everything, everything has been predicted several years before, and everything has come about, and much yet is left to come about.**

World War II. In undeniably clear terms, Jesus repeatedly told Luisa about the Second World War long before it happened. For example, we see the following words of Jesus to Luisa:

January 16, 1923: Ah! **it is the second general turmoil that the nations are preparing…** They should have understood [matters] by themselves, and been meeker toward the oppressed; on the contrary, they are more inexorable, wanting not only their humiliation, but also their destruction … more cities will be destroyed … *September 2, 1923*: Last year, France, by moving against Germany, rang the first bell. Italy, by moving against Greece, rang the second war bell. Then, another nation will come, which will ring the third, to call them to the fight. *November 16, 1926*: They are preparing fierce wars and revolutions. This time it will not be just Europe, but other races will unite together. The circle will be more extensive; other parts of the world will participate. …**But I will use this for my highest purposes, and *the reunion of so many races will serve to facilitate the communications* of the truths**, so that they may dispose themselves for the Kingdom of the Supreme Fiat. *March 31, 1927*: … while apparently it seems that they want to agree, in reality they are plotting new wars. … they are converting that peace, so praised with words, but not with deeds, into preparations for war. As you can already see, many different races have united to fight, some with one pretext, some with another—and more will unite together. But I will use the union of these races, because for the coming of the Kingdom of my Divine Will it is necessary to have the union of all **races by means of another war, much more extensive than the last one** … after the war, the diffusion of the Kingdom of my Will will be easier. *August 12, 1927*: What wickedness—after so many evils of a war they have gone through, they are preparing another one, more terrible, and they are trying to move almost the entire world, as if it were one single man.

Consider that the prophetic reality in the September 1923 message is found in Jesus' calling France's move "ringing the first bell." This statement makes no sense outside of understanding it as a harbinger of a coming conflict. We now know, in studying the buildup to World War II, that it is perfectly accurate to say that, in the 1920s, France did indeed "ring the first bell" with its unjust occupation and practices in Germany. But we can also see that Mussolini's imperial attempts in 1922 to create a "New Roman Empire" constituted the "second bell," as Jesus told Luisa. For in "moving against Greece" by formalizing control of the Greek Dodecanese Islands and ordering the invasion of Corfu (another Greek island), Mussolini created a conflict that contributed significantly to the deterioration of conditions which lead to World War II. **But what about this mysterious "third bell"?** Remember that Luisa received this message in 1923, long before anyone knew that Germany would suddenly explode onto the world stage and invade Poland in the following decade. That was all it took for World War II to begin: one more "bell," and only one more nation was needed to "ring" it. Clearly Germany fulfilled this role. Many other nations had parts to play, but no one denies that World War II began by Britain declaring war on Germany in 1939 in response to Germany's invasion of Poland. What is more, Jesus gave Luisa this "third bell" warning in September 1923— only two months before Hitler made his first major (failed) move, attempting militarily to seize power in Munich.

In the message from November 16, 1926, and March 31, 1927, Jesus also prophesied to Luisa the results of World War II; the unprecedented Globalization that would follow in the explosion of international trade and communications. He even said that He specifically allowed all the turmoil precisely in order to enable this Globalization, which in turn would allow for the dissemination of the knowledges necessary for the coming of the Kingdom.

Earthquakes and Volcanoes. On April 17th, 1906, Luisa was shown great chastisements; specifically, **earthquakes in three different cities.** We read:

> It seemed that the earth would open and threaten to swallow cities, mountains and men. It seemed that the Lord would want to destroy the earth, but **in a special way three different places, distant from one another, and some of them also in Italy**. … in some places the earth was opening and horrible quakes would occur. I could not understand very well whether these things were happening or will have to happen. How many ruins!

The very next day, the great San Francisco earthquake struck. According to the USGS, this "ranks as one of the most significant earthquakes of all time," and it remains the deadliest earthquake in American history. Three thousand people were killed and 80% of the city of San Francisco was destroyed. **Four months later**, the 1906 Valparaíso Earthquake occurred in Chile which killed even more people than the San Francisco quake. **Two years later,** the great Messina Earthquake wreaked havoc in Sicily (Italy) on December 28, 1908. It remains the worst and deadliest earthquake in European history. At least 80,000 people were killed (and perhaps up to 200,000), and the city of Messina (as well as Reggio Calabria) was destroyed. Luisa was also shown this earthquake several hours before it happened in the following message:

> I felt as if the earth were **shaking and wanted to slip away from beneath us**. I was concerned, and I said to myself: 'Lord, Lord, what is this?' And He, in my interior: "Earthquakes." And He kept silent. I almost paid no attention to Him, and within myself I continued my usual interior things when, all of a sudden, about five hours after that word had been spoken to me, I felt the earthquake sensibly [*note: her previous "feeling" of the earthquake was in her usual mystical state*]…I could see harrowing things… [and Jesus said:] 'I will destroy a great part of [the world], with earthquakes, with waters, and with wars.' (December 28, 1908)

Although one might say this particular entry lacks any prophetic value because Luisa could have made it up only after sensibly feeling the earthquake, this protestation fails to account for the fact that her words here (written, as they always were, very early in the day—before the priest came in at 6am to bless her and say Mass) clearly indicate a large earthquake, of which she could not have then been sensibly aware, as she was located 200 miles away from the epicenter and would have felt only light shaking (which could have simply felt like a nearby, but less powerful, earthquake). But, mere days later, Jesus had another stark message for Luisa, revealing that the disasters were anything but over:

> "Is the whole earth not in the palm of my hand? Could I perhaps not open chasms in the earth and cause them to be swallowed in other places as well? And to show them this, **I will cause earthquakes in other places, in which they do not usually occur."** While saying this, He seemed **to stretch out His hand into the center of the earth, taking some fire and moving it closer to the surface of the earth;** and the earth would shake and the earthquake would be felt, some places more intensely, some places less. (January 2, 1909)

Exactly three weeks after Jesus gave this message to Luisa, the infamous 1909 Borujerd earthquake struck Iran, killing 8,000. **Six months later, France—a region which scarcely ever suffers from any earthquakes—was struck by what remains to this day the largest earthquake ever recorded in its history** (the 1909 Provence earthquake). Within the mere few decades that followed this message, hundreds of thousands of people throughout the world died in earthquakes—a scale of earthquake-wrought devastation orders of magnitude beyond anything that had been seen in the world for hundreds of years.

Three years later, an astounding event occurred: the 20th century's largest volcanic eruption (only surpassed in size throughout all history by Tambora), which was a full *thirty times* as large as the famous eruption of Mt. St. Helens. But the truly amazing thing was that this eruption came out of nowhere; bursting forth from a spot in the ground (accompanied as it was by many simultaneous earthquakes) in Alaska where no volcano had previously existed, in fulfillment of what Luisa was shown three years earlier in the message above. This volcano is thus now fittingly called *Novarupta*, Latin for "newly erupted," but the area was so remote that a scientific expedition only arrived close to the true site four years after the eruption. Nevertheless, the expeditioners described it as a "modern inferno" saying that it was a "horrifying" sight with tens of thousands of jets of steam roaring from the still burning hot ash (which was up to 700 feet deep), such that it was "one of the most amazing visions ever beheld by mortal eye." The USGS (United States Geological Survey) is still amazed by the event due to it being accompanied by the "extreme seismicity" of 14 separate earthquakes and due to the dozens of associated phenomena that shattered the then-scientific consensuses of the day regarding the operation of volcanoes and earthquakes. To this day, however, scientists admit that the full story of the eruption is not fully understood, despite being a famous enigma for geologists and perhaps the most rigorously studied eruption in history. It seems the best explanation for the mystery shall remain what Luisa was shown above; that "some fire" was taken by God and "moved closer to the surface of the earth."

    <u>International Relations of the 20th Century.</u> Before even two months had passed after the dawn of the 20th century, Luisa did not hesitate to assert, **"Ah, yes, it really seemed that this century of ours will be renowned for its pride."** (February 19, 1900) Looking back, this is an obvious diagnosis, but in the very beginning of the 1900s it was far from apparent that the century then in its infancy would be known above all by the title of the deadliest of sins. For it *seemed* that a period of great prosperity, peace, and progress was in motion and destined to continue. The world was enjoying its 85th consecutive year of *Pax Britannica;* that period of apparent peace with no major wars between the Great Powers of the world during which the unprecedented imperial influence of the British Empire gave stability to much of the world (while of course, as we know now, committing many atrocities). The Congress of Vienna was still in force, and the Napoleonic Wars (the last major European conflicts before World War I) had become scarcely even a memory among the centenarians of that time. Amazing new technologies—especially seen in transportation and communication—were making life easier than it ever had been and were opening new opportunities of which people had never previously dreamed. It seemed that the "public mood" had never been higher. And yet in Luisa's revelations, we see the following:

> July 3rd, 1900: Yet, my daughter, the chastisements I am sending are still nothing compared to those which have been prepared. July 25th, 1900: [Luisa writes:] Jesus came and made me see **a machine in which it seemed that many human members were being crushed, as well as something like two signs of chastisements in the air, which were terrifying.** October 22nd, 1900: [Luisa writes:] If the many chastisements about which I wrote in these books should really happen, who would have the heart to be spectator of them? And the blessed Lord made me comprehend with clarity that some of them will take place while I am still on this earth [the first half of the 20th century], some after my death… January 2, 1909: [Jesus says:] 'This is only the beginning of the chastisements…'

Recall that at the time of these messages, military technology remained largely as it had been for many decades. But World War I, 14 years later, saw the incredible advance of horrendous and lethal new weaponry. Luisa was likely shown one of these new weapons in the July 25th message above. (One also wonders if the two "terrifying signs of chastisements in the air" mentioned therein were the atomic bombs dropped on Japan. For this message was given to Luisa exactly 45 years before the eve of the July 26, 1945 issuance of the Potsdam Declaration, which, with the atomic bombs as its inspiration, promised "prompt and utter destruction" for Japan in the absence of "unconditional surrender.")

But after World War I, we see messages equally prophetic regarding the continuation of the evil nature of the century. This, too, is noteworthy, because after the end of this so-called "War to End All Wars," many thought lasting peace was finally at hand. Consider what H.G. Wells—the secular world's idea of a "prophet"—said at that time about World War I: "*This is ... a war not of nations, but of mankind. It is a war to exorcise a world-madness and end an age ... It aims at a settlement that shall stop this sort of thing for ever ... This, the greatest of all wars, is not just another war—it is the last war!*"[16] But Jesus made it clear to Luisa that this was not so. We already know this from the prophecies that specifically spoke of World War II, quoted above, but here is what He said to Luisa during World War I:

> November 20th, 1914 [In World War I's opening months, Luisa writes:] Jesus keeps telling me that **the wars and the scourges which are occurring now, are still nothing**, while it seems that they are too much; that other nations will go to war—and not only this, but that they will wage war against the Church, attack sacred people and kill them ... October 16th, 1918 (Close to the end of this war): I will renew the world with the sword, with fire and with water, with sudden deaths, and with contagious diseases. I will make new things. **The nations will form a sort of tower of Babel**; they will reach the point of being unable to understand one another; the peoples will revolt among themselves; they will no longer want kings. All will be humiliated, and peace will come only from Me. And **if you hear them say 'peace', that will not be true, but apparent**. June 18, 1925: [Jesus says:] All things will be turned upside down. Many new phenomena will occur, such as to confuse the pride of man; wars, revolutions, mortalities of every kind will not be spared.

With the words of Mr. Wells resounding loudly in the ears of all, the League of Nations was triumphantly formed. A historically unprecedented international organization, explicitly established to ensure world peace, was sure—they thought—to succeed in its stated aim. But Jesus here tells Luisa that it was a mere "tower of Babel." And indeed, it proved itself just that; an opportunity for much babbling, while delivering on none of its promises of the preservation of peace.

<u>The Abuse Crisis of the Church</u>. In His revelations to Luisa, **Jesus goes so far as to say that the hierarchy of the Church had become so corrupt that the very enemies of the Church were necessary in order to purge and purify her.** Indeed, today, it is sometimes the Church's avowed enemies who are doing what the Bishops should have done long ago: dealing with the sin of sexual abuse as strongly as it should be dealt with and exposing the perpetrators. Even Pope Francis and Pope Benedict XVI themselves have openly stated that the revelations of the abuse crisis have been a needed purification, and that the secular investigators and journalists have done the right thing in exposing the pervasive rot among so many of the clergy. But Jesus' words to Luisa here are a full 100 years before their time (and one can only wonder if it was words like these—and other strong criticisms of the

hierarchy Jesus voiced to Luisa—that encouraged the condemnation of her writings; despite how accurate and called for all now know them to be). In the following passage, Jesus prophesies today's crisis to Luisa decades before it began; although He does not explicitly refer to the crisis as involving sexual abuse, it is safe to say that this may be the primary thing He intended when He specifically spoke to Luisa of the *false virtuous* being protected and the *true good* being condemned by the very Bishops themselves, while the *children* suffer *injustice* and the *secular* are *induced by God Himself to rail against* these corrupt Bishops—a perfect description of the hidden crimes in the Church of the latter half of the 20th century and the following just fury of the first two decades of the 21st:

> [Luisa writes:] I was praying blessed Jesus to confound the enemies of the Church, and my always lovable Jesus... told me: "My daughter, **I could confound the enemies of the Holy Church**, but I don't want to. **If I did so, who would purge my Church?** The members of the Church, and especially **those who occupy positions and heights of dignity, have their eyes dazzled, and they blunder a great deal, reaching the point of protecting the false virtuous and oppressing and condemning the true good**. This grieves Me so much—to see those few true **children of mine under the weight of injustice...** This grieves Me so much, that I **feel I am all fury for their sake!** Listen my daughter, I am all sweetness, benign, clement and merciful...But I am also strong, as to be able to crush and reduce to ashes those who ... oppress the good... Ah! you cry over the secular, and I cry over the painful wounds which are in the body of the Church. **These grieve Me so much as to surpass the wounds of the secular... and induce Me to make the secular rail against them.** (May 16, 1911)

Mussolini's March on Rome. In a prophecy given the very day before a certain major historical event took place, Jesus told Luisa:

> They want to gamble away Rome...even the Italians, want to gamble her away... See, people pop out from all sides, to join together and storm her; and, what's more, under the guises of lambs, while they are rapacious wolves that want to devour the prey. (October 27, 1922)

This is exactly what happened *the next day* when fascist troops under Benito Mussolini entered Rome. Instead of defending her, the King (Victor Emmanuel III) simply handed power over to them without conflict; thus, as Jesus said, "gambling away Rome." (Jesus of course knew that within this insurrection laid in wait destructive plans which eventually materialized into the Second World War, hence His severe lamentations in this passage.) This gamble tragically placed the Vatican State geographically within a political entity being ruled by Fascists—but the King did not care, not seeing Fascism as a threat to his comfortable establishment. Of course, Mussolini had indeed threatened to take Rome three days earlier. But this message Luisa received on the 27th of October contains much more than a mere worry about Rome being taken; rather, it includes a lamentation about Rome being *"gambled away,"* which only God (and perhaps King Victor) knew would happen. Even the prime minister himself (Luigi Facta) assumed this gamble would not happen—proven by his declaration of Martial Law—in order to allow for Rome to be militarily defended against the march, a declaration the King later refused to sign. Indeed, there is no explanation of this passage other than the admission of its prophetic nature.

St. Hannibal's Exaltation. There are well over a billion Catholics in the world today; presumably, each is striving to be a canonized saint (if only!). Nevertheless, the number of saints who are actually canonized compared to the number of Catholics who are quite holy and doubtless worthy of the honor is so utterly minimal as to be almost negligible by any statistical standard. And of the many holy people whom Luisa knew—and of the countless people she exhorted to *become* saints—she only referred to one *as* a saint: Fr. Hannibal di Francia. Now, we have all referred to people as saints, no doubt, and time will prove all of us wrong (as far as canonization is concerned, that is). But it did not prove Luisa wrong. Fr. Hannibal was indeed canonized 57 years after Luisa's own death; and, not only that, but Jesus also told Luisa that Fr. Hannibal would be the first promoter of the Divine Will to be glorified (despite countless people around Luisa being utterly convicted of her mission and likewise working hard to promote her works). The very day Fr. Hannibal died, Luisa wrote:

> I was feeling very afflicted…because I had received the unexpected news of the death of Reverend **Father Di Francia**. He was the only one left to me, to whom I could open my poor soul. **How well he could understand me—it was to a saint that I would entrust myself** … *he was a saint* … And now, Jesus has taken him to Heaven. [And, several months after Fr. Hannibal died, Jesus told Luisa:] Do you think that the memory of Father Di Francia, his many sacrifices and desires to make my Will known, to the point of initiating the publication, will be extinguished in this great work of my Divine Fiat, only because I brought him with Me to Heaven? No, no; on the contrary, he will have the first place … He prepared the ground so that my Divine Will might be known; so much so, that he spared nothing, neither expenses, nor sacrifices… when this great work becomes known, his name, his memory, will be full of glory and of splendor… (February 28, 1928)

***

What have we seen so far in this Chapter? We have seen that Luisa's revelations are beyond doubt Heaven-sent: her 81 years of saintly living prove this, her miracles prove this, her legacy proves this, the success of her cause proves this, her prophecies prove this, and her intercession from Heaven even now proves this. But we have also seen that sure prophecies of the Era are not restricted to her revelations, but rather permeate Church History—in the teachings of the Fathers, the Magisterium of the Popes, and in the multitudes of trustworthy private revelations given to the faithful— to such an extent that to doubt them would require such an absurd degree of incredulity that it even risks reducing Faith in God to mere Philosophical Deism.

There is so much more I wish to tell you about what is coming: how this Era will fit perfectly upon the whole history of the world as its crown; how the sanctity of the Church for the last 2,000 years has been preparing for the Gift that is the essence of the Era; how, ever since the Fall of Man, God has been busy at work in all of His greatest interventions preparing the way for the Gift and the Era. And we will get to all of that in Chapters 3 and 4, but at this point I simply cannot justify delaying—even one more minute—telling you what you need to know in order to get to work in hastening this Era, as each of us should now be filled with an intense desire for its arrival.

For what Jesus tells Luisa contains not mere news of this impending event, but a *call*, against which we mustn't cover our ears, to hasten the Era. And the call to do so consists in this: receiving the greatest gift possible—His very own Divine Will as our own will. Only with this Gift can we really work to hasten the Era for which we all so long. Let us, then, get to work, and turn our attention to that very task in the following chapter, after which we will consider more closely why the Era must come and why now is the proper time for its arrival.

†✝†

Chapter 2: What Should I Do to Hasten the Era?

It is indeed time for us to get to work. But to do so requires we step back and consider, as deeply as possible, the very question that, more so than any other, no human being on earth can evade: **what is the meaning of life?** Knowing that existence itself foists upon us the duty to stop at nothing in striving to answer it, men and women of all times and places have zealously sought to answer this question. But today, they often grow only more confused in undertaking this search; wrought as it always is with all manner of philosophical and theological error. Therefore, at the end of their inquiry, they find themselves worse off than when they boldly embarked upon it, thus becoming jaded or even cynical. Let us now put an end to both the cynicism and the confusion with one fell swoop.

Consider the Meaning of Life

All believers know that our *ultimate end*—that which, above all, we hope and strive to attain—is Heaven. "The End of man is Heaven," Jesus said frankly to Luisa on April 4, 1931, reiterating St. Augustine's own most famous teaching in his *Confessions: "Thou hast made us for Thyself, Lord, and our hearts are restless 'till they rest in Thee."*

But it does not follow that Heaven is the "meaning of life" in the sense of being the *natural* end of man, in addition to being man's *ultimate* (and supernatural) end. As the authoritative *New Catholic Encyclopedia* states in its article entirely devoted to this very conundrum, "…**there is not yet a completely satisfactory resolution of this problem** …" Strange as it is that such an important question still does not have a "satisfactory resolution," God had a plan in allowing this delay. **Jesus' revelations to Luisa give the resolution to this problem.** Although Heaven indeed is our ultimate end—our destiny— it is not a due perfection *in* our nature. This is simply to say that Heaven is, rather, a completely *gratuitous* gift from God; not a "just payment" (for giving that which nature demands is always a *just payment*, not a *gratuitous gift*). Making this distinction is anything but theological hair-splitting, for **what is due in our nature itself is also that which Adam must have enjoyed before the Fall, it is that to which mankind must return before the end of time, and it is that in which our meaning of life presently consists.**

Some theologians still cling to the notion that Heaven itself is not only the ultimate end of man, but is also man's *natural* end. Venerable Pope Pius XII, however, taught clearly in his encyclical *Humani Generis* (§ 26) that this is an error: "*Others destroy the gratuity of the supernatural order, since God, they say, cannot create intellectual beings without ordering and calling them to the beatific vision.*" The Pope is here teaching, in other words, that God didn't *have to* order us toward Heaven itself—His choice to do so was pure gratuity. But God *does have to* create beings with all their due perfections, lest He be guilty of creating an evil (the very definition of which is "the absence of a due perfection," (cf. *Summa Theologica.* I, Q49, A1.)), which can never be so. Consequently, Heaven cannot be our nature's due perfection.

What, then, *is* our due perfection? What is our "good"—that is, our "natural end"? Well, the good of any individual thing always consists in the greatest power of that thing being completely dominated by the corresponding power of a being of a higher nature. Accordingly, the "good," or "natural end," of any musical instrument is to have its musical potency (its greatest power as a physical object) actualized by an expert musician, with the instrument itself providing no impediment to the musician's skill, but rather beautifully incarnating the same. The good of a plant is to have its fruit (the generation of which is its own greatest power) be consumed and digested by a sentient being (whether man or animal), such that the matter of this fruit becomes so dominated by this sentient being that it is incorporated into the body of the latter. The good of an animal is to be perfectly obedient with its own sentience (its greatest power) to man and to serve the latter; for example, one observes most clearly the natural end of an animal in a domesticated service dog who obeys his master perfectly, and no animals on the face of the planet achieve so great a dignity as those search and rescue dogs that even save human lives. **Finally, the natural end, or good, of man is to have his own greatest faculty—his will—be totally dominated by the corresponding power of *the* Higher Being: the Will of God. In other words, the natural end of man is not only becoming a saint (it is indeed that), but becoming the *greatest* saint possible by receiving the *Crown* of Sanctity, which is none other than the Gift of Living in the Divine Will.**

While no serious arguments exist that the body and its passions (or even the soul's memory), is man's greatest faculty, some theologians do insist that it is not the will, but the intellect, that holds the supremacy in man. Granted, the intellect is indeed the endowment of man that primarily separates him from the beasts (man can be defined as "*rational* animal") and holds the chronological primacy (as the axiom says, "nothing can be loved unless it is first known"), but it is nevertheless clearly the will that is the greatest power of the soul. It is the will that especially corresponds to the greatest virtue, charity. It is the will that *chooses whether* to pursue the good after the intellect informs the will of its discovery regarding *what is* good. It is the will that commands the intellect to submit to a known truth after the intellect presents it to the will. As Frank Sheed says, "Salvation depends directly upon the will," (*Theology and Sanity*), not upon the intellect. Another axiom rightly teaches that "the corruption of the greatest is the worst," and from this we can conclude that the will must be the greatest among the soul's powers, since no one denies that its own corruption is the worst fate a soul can possibly suffer (as it is even worse to hate God—that is, for the will's disposition toward Him to be corrupted—than it is to hold errors in one's intellect regarding Him). "All merit lies in the will," as Jesus Himself said to St. Faustina (*Diary* §1760). And, as Pope Benedict XVI taught, "the primacy of will sheds light on the fact that God is charity before all else... 'Eternal life is simply the desire as well as the will to love, blessed and perfect.'" (Apostolic Letter. October 28, 2008)

To receive the Gift is the meaning of life. **It is that simple.** Let us, therefore, spare no expense to receive this Gift. Only with It can we hasten the Era. Only with It can we achieve the meaning of life. Within It is everything; with It we lack nothing.

> The height of freedom is the 'yes,' in conformity with God's will. It is only in the 'yes' that man truly becomes himself; only in the great openness of the 'yes,' in the unification of his will with the divine, that man becomes immensely open, becomes 'divine'... It is by transferring the human will to the divine will that the real person is born... –Pope Benedict XVI. (General Audience. June 25th, 2008)

Receive the Gift: The Crown of Sanctity

We began this book with "The Story of You," and there I relayed what the prophecies truly indicate your life will be like during the Era. But there was one thing I did not tell you in that section: *you can live that life right now.* Not, admittedly, in all its external details; many of those can only come with the Era itself, when there will be no more temptation to focus on externals at the expense of inner beauty. But the most important part—in fact, all that *really* matters—can be lived now, for at the end of the day all that matters is our sanctity. Sanctity alone builds up treasures within our only ultimate destiny (which is Heaven, not the Era), and the great sanctity of the Era can be lived right now, by anyone. So, although we are already well into this book, we have now arrived at the real crux of the matter, and the duty which stands before us outshines all other duties. Let us, therefore, strive above all else to receive this new sanctity (and while I hope that the next several pages prove helpful, I have covered the matter more thoroughly in pages 198-290 of *The Crown of Sanctity*). Furthermore, living this sanctity now is how the Era will come about: only when enough people are already living this life of sanctity on earth will Heaven grant its own life to earth and thereby allow the universal fruits of the sanctity to be bestowed upon the entire world externally. **This sanctity is called the Gift of Living in the Divine Will. Receiving this Gift is more necessary than necessity itself, and the following sections will enable you to receive It.**

Follow the Three Necessary Preliminary Steps

First, we must believe and heed the fundamental truths with conviction and the certainty of Faith. And the truth is this: There is a God. This God became a man, Jesus Christ. This Jesus founded a Church on Peter, to whom He gave authority and keys— keys that have been handed down continuously for 2,000 years to Peter's current successor. (Please see *The Crown of Sanctity* pages 24-48 if you could use any help understanding and heeding these truths.) Above all, both believe and heed *every single word* of the Catechism.

Second, we must strive to be rid of all sin. To live a sinful life is to oppose the Era, not to herald it. Let us, therefore, examine our consciences carefully. In the Gospel, Jesus' first admonition upon the initiation of His public ministry was simple; "Repent, for the Kingdom of Heaven is at hand." (Matthew 4:17) He says the same to us today with even more emphasis, as the total earthly fulfillment of that Kingdom He preached 2,000 years ago is now upon us with immediacy. I do not wish to include within the pages of this short book a lengthy treatment of ridding one's life of sin, but I encourage anyone who could use guidance in this process to read pages 197-203 in *The Crown of Sanctity*.

Third, we must desire and pursue sanctity above all other things. The Gift of Living in the Divine Will is the *Crown* of Sanctity, not a *substitution* for sanctity. It presupposes that we pursue "ordinary" sanctity with all the vigor of our ancestors in the Faith. Perhaps the most important part of this pursuit of sanctity is **the renunciation of the self-will:** with the Gift, we are asking the Divine Will to reign in us, and two wills cannot *reign* in one soul. The renunciation of the self-will necessary for receiving the Gift is the same renunciation that has always been taught by the spiritual masters (see, for example, the works of St. Francis de Sales, St. Alphonsus Liguori, and St. Thérèse of Lisieux—some of whose teachings are relayed in Chapter 3 of this book); so, although renunciation deserves a whole chapter of its own, I will remain content leaving you with this reference instead of writing one.

"There is only one tragedy, ultimately: not to have been a saint" –Pope Francis. *Gaudete et Exsultate.*
(Quoting Leon Bloy.)

Desire and Ask for The Gift

Regarding the Gift Itself, we have thus far done little more than name It and refer to It. In order to truly desire It, we must better understand what It is and what astounding graces come with It, in accordance with the axiom quoted above which also reminds us that *what is known more can be loved more*. **So, what is this Gift?** It is the "New and Divine Holiness" promoted by Pope St. John Paul II, the *continuous participation in the Trinity's one eternal operation*; the *full actualization of the soul's powers*; the *sharing in God's prime motion*; the *Divine and Eternal Mode of holiness*; the *Real Life of Jesus in the soul.* But what exactly does this mean?

It means the sanctity of Our Lady; for, while she shall always remain by far the greatest creature due to her Sovereign Privileges, she nevertheless more than happily mediates to us her very own sanctity now that the time for it has arrived. She, indeed, is truly the quintessence of Living in the Divine Will and our model for It. For her dignity far surpasses that of Adam and Eve (who were created with the Gift in force), and, furthermore, she remains a creature unlike her Divine Son. Through Our Lady, God demonstrates just what marvels of sanctity He is capable of working in a created human being. In Luisa's revelations, we learn that it is not God's Will that *only* Mary remain in such a lofty state of sanctity, merely for us to gaze upon from a nearly infinitely inferior position. On the contrary, it is His Will that we, too, rise up to her sanctity, so that it can even be said of us, as it has long been rightly said of her by St. Louis de Montfort and so many others, that *one of our acts can give God more glory and surpass in merit all the acts of all other saints combined.*[17]

It means our own acts becoming reflections of her perfect and quintessential Fiat, so that, as Our Lady's "Fiat" preceded the very Incarnation itself, so our "Fiats" may, as it were, cause as many incarnations as acts we undertake. If ordinary virtuous acts build up treasures of mansions and mountains in Heaven, then these acts *in the Divine Will* build up treasures of cities and continents.

It means the perfect fulfillment of the Our Father prayer: "Thy Will be done on earth as It is in Heaven." That is to say, It consists in living *the very life* of the Blessed in Heaven as far as holiness is concerned, while still retaining that which is intrinsic to life on earth— the absence of the Beatific Vision, the continued presence of the Veil (and the concomitant need for living by Faith), and the ability to suffer.

And why, more specifically, should you desire the Gift? Even a brief glance at a few promises that come with It from Jesus' revelations to Luisa make this clear. **Within It your complete happiness is assured.**

As the soul enters into my Volition… [she] lives of Heaven, nor is there any room for miseries and for unhappinesses. My light destroys everything, and it transforms evils into good. (May 7, 1933) We want to see her happy—and of Our own happiness. (September 21, 1931) Those who will possess [the Divine Will and the knowledges thereof] will have the source of light, of sanctity; therefore, darkness, weaknesses, the ugliness of sin, poverty in divine goods, will end for them. All evils will end, and they will possess the source of Sanctity. (October 19, 1926) It is the nature of my Will to make happiness, joy and Paradise arise, wherever It reigns. Will of God and unhappiness does not exist, nor can exist. (January 30, 1927)

Within It you have what even the saints in Heaven envy.

[In a letter, Luisa writes:] To love in the Divine Will astonishes Heaven and earth; the very Saints yearn to have within their hearts this conquering Love of one who lives in exile [that is, the grace of one who can still acquire merit by virtue of the ability to suffer].

Within It is such spiritual strength that no burden can trouble you.

One who possesses my Divine Will has ... the divine strength; and if he were told to lift the heavy object, without becoming troubled, he takes it as if it were nothing ... one who has my Divine Will has sufficient strength for anything; so, everything is easy for her; even suffering, as she feels strong, she looks at it as a new gain. (July 30, 1929)

Within It alone can you build up as many treasures in Heaven as possible.

Each act done on earth [in the Divine Will] will be like taking more room in Heaven, one additional right, and an advanced possession of the celestial dwelling ... My Divine Fiat never says 'enough' to the creature... (June 8, 1931)

Within It alone is our built-up treasure truly invincible.

Each thought, word, pain suffered, everything, [in the Divine Will] remains written and Sealed with Indelible characters. Perhaps the memory does not keep track of everything, it has forgotten many things, but the will hides everything and loses nothing such that it is the depositary of all of her acts. (March 19, 1933)

Within It is superabundant eternal rewards forever for each act.

When the soul, then, fusing herself in Me, does her immediate acts with Me, then I feel so drawn toward her that I do what she does together with her, and I transmute the operating of the creature into divine. I take everything into account, and I reward everything, even the smallest things; and even just one good act of the will does not remain defrauded in the creature. (March 28, 1917)

Within It is an anchor of your very salvation itself.

The acts done in my Divine Will are everlasting and inseparable from God... And even if [the soul] goes wandering, she feels the irresistible need, the strong chains that pull her into the arms of her Creator. This happened to Adam, because the beginning of his life was lived in my Divine Will. Even though he sinned, was cast out of Eden, went wandering for all his life—yet, was he perhaps lost? Ah no! ... You cannot comprehend all the good and what it means to operate in Our Will. By operating in It, the soul acquires as many pledges of infinite value for as many acts as she does in Our Fiat; and these pledges remain in God Himself ... Therefore, do not fear, the acts done in Our Will are eternal bonds, chains not subject to breaking. ... do not want to trouble the peace of your heart; abandon yourself in Me, and do not fear. (April 16, 1931)

Within It is deliverance from any time in Purgatory.

The first thing that my Will does is to get Purgatory out of the way, making the creature go through It in advance, so as to be more free to let her live in It and to form Its life as It best pleases. So, if the creature dies after an act, determined and wanted, of wanting to live in my Volition, she will take flight toward Heaven. (October 27, 1935)

Within It is the transformation of your past.

As the creature decides with immutable firmness to want to Live of My Will ... It covers everything that she has done up to then with My Will. It molds them, It Transforms them into Its Light in a way that everyone sees, with the Prodigy of Its Transforming Love, that everything is Its Will in the creature. (November 3, 1936) [*Note: Jesus is not saying that objective acts of the past themselves change; indeed, that would be a logical absurdity and impossibility—but rather that their relation to eternity (which is all that matters) is transformed with the Gift.*]

We could easily continue this section for many more pages, but who at this point could have anything but overwhelming desire for the Gift? These few paragraphs contain only a small preview: dive into Luisa's writings and you will not leave them without this burning desire for the Gift re-inflamed in your heart. **From this desire for His Will and the renunciation of our own, we are prepared to receive the Gift. Let us now ask for It.**

Asking for the Gift is as simple as it sounds. **When it comes to this step, there are no magical formulas to be memorized or Gnostic secrets into which one need be initiated.** Have we perhaps forgotten that God hears each thing we say, every moment of every day? That He is ever closer to us than our own skin? No special strategies are needed to "reach Him." He is right next to you. Like a child, simply ask Him for what you desire. Jesus tells Luisa:

> As the creature truly decides that she wants to live in my Divine Will, and at any cost never to do her own, my Fiat, with an unspeakable love, forms the seed of Its life in the depth of the soul. (October 27, 1935) The first indispensable thing in order to enter into my Fiat is wanting and yearning with all firmness to live in It... The second thing is to take the first step ... **See then, how easy it is, but it is necessary to want it... I hold nothing back when it comes to making the creature live in my Will** (May 6, 1938) How many Gifts do We want to give! But because they are not asked for, We retain Them ... waiting to give Them when they are asked for. (March 20, 1932)

Just ask!!! What matters is not so much *how* you ask, but *that* you ask. What matters is that you do not allow yourself to *forget* to ask. What matters is that you ask *continuously*. **Say, as much as you possibly can, "Jesus, I Trust in You. Thy Will be done." And "I give you my will, please give me Yours in return."**

Now, despite how truly simple this matter is, formal vocal prayers can here (as everywhere) be a great help, and these are certainly not lacking in asking for the Gift. I will only share a couple here, but there are many beautiful Divine Will prayers to be found; please see the appendices of *The Crown of Sanctity*, or simply do an internet search if you would like more.

A prayer for each morning. (A Prevenient Act):

Good morning, Blessed Mother, I love you. Come, help me to offer my first act of the day as an act of love in the Divine Will of God. Most Holy Trinity, I thank and praise you for this new day. Setting my will in Yours, I affirm I want only to live and act in Your Will, and I set all of my acts of the day in order in You. O Jesus, through, with, and in the Immaculate Heart of Mary, I consecrate and give my will to You in exchange for Your Divine Will. I truly want Your Divine Will to generate Its Divine Life in me this day—to think in all my thoughts, to speak in all my words, and operate in all my actions for the glory of our Heavenly Father and to fulfill the purpose of Creation. Abandoned in Your arms, my Jesus, I invite all the angels and saints, especially Mary Most Holy, to join in all the Divine Will does in me today, and I am confident that You will not fail to give me the grace to be always faithful and attentive to Your action within me so that my own will dare not interfere with Your freedom to form Your Real Life in me. O my Jesus, I love You with Your own Will and thank You profoundly for the knowledge and Gift of the Divine Will. Amen.

Prayer of Consecration to the Divine Will *(Composed by Luisa at the request of St. Hannibal):*

O adorable and Divine Will, here I am, before the immensity of Your Light, that Your eternal Goodness may open to me the doors, and make me enter into It, to form my life all in You, Divine Will. Therefore, prostrate before Your Light, I, the littlest among all creatures, come, O adorable Will, into the little group of the first children of Your Supreme Fiat. Prostrate in my nothingness, I beseech and implore Your endless Light, that It may want to invest me and eclipse everything that does not belong to You, in such a way that I may do nothing other than look, comprehend and live in You, Divine Will. It will be my life, the center of my intelligence, the enrapturer of my heart and of my whole being. In this heart the human will will no longer have life; I will banish it forever, and will form the new Eden of peace, of happiness and of love. With It I shall always be happy, I shall have a unique strength, and a sanctity that sanctifies everything and brings everything to God. Here prostrate, I invoke the help of the Sacrosanct Trinity, that They admit me to live in the cloister of the Divine Will, so as to restore in me the original order of Creation, just as the creature was created. Celestial Mother, Sovereign Queen of the Divine Fiat, take me by the hand and enclose me in the Light of the Divine Will. You will be my guide, my tender Mother; You will guard your child, and will teach me to live and to maintain myself in the order and in the bounds of the Divine Will. Celestial Sovereign, to your Heart I entrust my whole being; I will be the tiny little child of the Divine Will. You will teach me the Divine Will, and I will be attentive in listening to You. You will lay your blue mantle over me, so that the infernal serpent may not dare to penetrate into this Sacred Eden to entice me and make me fall into the maze of the human will. Heart of my highest Good, Jesus, You will give me Your flames, that they may burn me, consume me and nourish me, to form in me the life of the Supreme Will. Saint Joseph, You will be my Protector, the Custodian of my heart, and will keep the keys of my will in Your hands. You will keep my heart jealously, and will never give it to me again, that I may be sure never to go out of the Will of God. Guardian Angel, guard me, defend me, help me in everything, so that my Eden may grow flourishing, and be the call of the whole world into the Will of God. Celestial Court, come to my help, and I promise You to live always in the Divine Will. Amen.

Grow in the Virtues

To be continuously anchored in the Gift, we must be virtuous. But we should also recall that Christ's burden is light, and His yoke is easy. (cf. Matthew 11:30) Virtue is not difficult, and Jesus reiterates this to Luisa, saying:

> **My daughter, they say that the path of virtue is difficult. False.** It is difficult for one who does not move, because knowing neither the graces nor the consolations she would receive from God, nor the help for her to move, it seems difficult to her; and without moving she feels all the weight of the journey. But **for one who moves, it is extremely easy, because the grace that inundates her fortifies her.** (May 15, 1905)

Haven't we all found this to be true? When we sit down to merely think about a task, it seems tremendous, and too often we cower in our rooms trembling at the sheer thought of it. But when we ignore these thoughts and simply get to work, we find things proceeding much more smoothly than we would have imagined. Oh, how much we underestimate God, Who always inundates us with His grace—making easy anything we need to do in order to carry out His Will, no matter how difficult it appears at first. For, contrary to the errors of the Pelagians, the grace to be virtuous comes from Divine Intervention, not as some simple consequence of a studious expertise of the virtues (perhaps this is why the experts in virtue themselves are often the ones most lacking in that very thing—as anyone unfortunate enough to be acquainted with an Ethicist or a Moral Theologian knows!) Therefore, set out! Get to work! Follow your calling. Engage wholeheartedly in your mission and approach your whole life as a mission from God. *You know what your mission is* (but if you need some suggestions, just read the following sections!). The grace to be virtuous will come amid your faithful undertaking of the Will of God for your life. In a word, as Jesus says: *move!*

Nevertheless, with these admonitions being stated and, I hope, remaining on the forefront of your mind, let us briefly consider some important individual virtues for Living in the Divine Will. Truly, the virtues for the Gift are just the virtues that have always been associated with sanctity, thus we have essentially covered this step with the third "Preliminary Step" mentioned previously. Here, I simply wish to draw attention to some virtues that are particularly emphasized by Jesus to Luisa.

Perfect Love. Simply put, we mustn't even think about ever allowing a single word or deed to proceed from our wills that is not, in its own way, an act of love (of God, and of neighbor—in that order). Jesus tells Luisa:

> My daughter, **Love and Will of God are on par** with each other, they never separate, and they form one single Life... if you do my Will, you will love, and if you love you place my Will in safety within you... (October 20, 1935) The most essential and necessary thing in a soul is charity ... (October 29, 1900) My Divine Will is light, love is heat. Light and heat are inseparable from each other, and form the same life... (May 21, 1929)

It is impossible to overemphasize the importance of love. "God is love," (1 John 4:8) as Scripture teaches, and, as Jesus said in the Gospel, the whole law is summed up in loving God and neighbor (cf. Matthew 22:37-40). We must recall that love is an act of the will—not an emotion. You cannot control how you feel, but you can control what you *will*, as Jesus says to Luisa:

> Don't you know that all you should care about is to do my Will and know whether you are in It? ... **Your Jesus never** looks **at what the creature feels**; many times feelings can deceive her. But rather, I look at her will and what she really wants—and that is what I take. (May 15, 1938) Ah, [the most glorious souls in Heaven] were not the ones who had done great things, penances, miracles ... **Love alone is what surpasses everything, and leaves everything behind. So, it is one who loves much, not one who does much, that will be more pleasing to the Lord.** (October 16, 1906)

Self-forgetfulness, Nothingness, and Humility. As St. Faustina says, humility is "nothing but the truth." But the truth is that, no matter how seemingly "great" we become, compared to God we are nothing. And if only we can recognize that, then receiving the Gift of Living in the Divine Will shall prove a smooth path. For we will then forget ourselves (why remember a nothing?), and once we have forgotten ourselves, we have attained the perfection of humility. This need for recognizing our nothingness is neither a Quietistic nor an Eastern Pantheistic practice; it is, rather, what St. Thérèse of Lisieux repeatedly insisted upon. For example, she wrote: "This enlightenment on my nothingness does me more good, in fact, than enlightenment on matters of faith. (*Story of a Soul* Ch. 9) It is enough to acknowledge our nothingness, and like children surrender ourselves into the Arms of the Good God. (Letter VI)" Instead of thinking and talking about ourselves (which are the primary acts contrary to this virtue of nothingness), we should live our lives like a tiger in the pursuit of its prey; so fixated upon its mission that a war could be raging on all sides of it and it would scarcely notice. Our mission is the salvation of souls, the hastening of the coming of the Kingdom of the Divine Will, and the consolation of our Blessed Lord. Our calling is the greatest calling possible. For us to spend time thinking about and talking about ourselves is more lamentable than a marine who, upon being sent on a mission of utmost importance to help end a war, instead stops for sightseeing in the city into which he was sent. This virtue, of course, does not preclude the need for a nightly examination of conscience (and a particularly careful one before Confession), but it does mean that we should avoid going much beyond that.

Attentiveness. Jesus constantly emphasizes this virtue to Luisa; for God does not waste one second. He understands much better than we do just how incredibly precious this short amount of time is that we spend as pilgrims on earth. Therefore, He is always at work molding us into great saints, but this cannot be successful if we refuse to be attentive to this endeavor of His as it plays out in each of our day's moments. The circumstances of life that are out of our control are quasi Divine Revelations: they speak to us about what God wills for us, and if—instead of listening to them—we get caught up in our own ideas about how our life (even our growth in holiness) should be transpiring, then the Gift may just sail us by. Another vital aspect of attentiveness is exercising care, prayerfulness, and good intentions, amid good works instead of letting these works become merely dry, habitual, reluctant, "check-off-the-box" type, solely external activities (cf. September 6, 1905). This does not mean we have to do everything slowly, but it does mean that we must resist the temptation to become like robots— undertaking even our good deeds with an ever-present demeanor of hasty distraction or even agitation, which robs them of value in God's sight.

Discernment. God is not like some referee at a sports game whose only job is to call out fouls or other violations when they occur; He is closer to each of us than our own selves, and what a crime when we treat Him as a mere arbiter! Jesus tells Luisa:

> They think that not doing my Will is something trivial, but instead, it is the total ruin of the creature … In order to be sure [of the faithfulness of people], I let them know that I want some little sacrifices … But if they are reluctant, everything will be upset in them, and all evils will swoop down upon them. Therefore, **not doing My Will is always an evil**-more or less grave, depending on the knowledge of It that one possesses. (April 8, 1927)

What follows, therefore, is the grave importance of trying to discern—so that we may both know and do—the Will of God in all things, instead of erroneously supposing that, so long as we are not blatantly sinning and are instead choosing between objectively good options, God has no Will in the matter. Now, these words of Jesus should not cause in us a sort of paralysis whereby we fear making decisions unless we know with clarity God's Will—that clarity itself is often not His Will! The point is, we must always be sincerely *trying*—in all things small and great—to do His Will. We ought not be afraid, either, to ask God for signs to indicate His Will for us in those cases where doing so is called for (and so long as we do not become superstitious). Additionally, we should remember that successful discernment can only proceed from the foundation of the principles of orthodox teaching, so we must be sure to never give "discernment" sufficient leeway to contradict these; it never can licitly do so, and when we pretend we can discern our way out of these orthodox principles, we are not discerning at all, but are rather dialoguing with the devil himself, just like Eve in the Garden.

Major decisions, for which the Will of God has not yet been made clear to us, should (whenever possible) be preceded by a novena for the grace to know and do God's Will.

(It is not that God is any less eager to answer our brief and spontaneous prayers; it is simply that God knows how very weak our memories are, and that, absent a novena, we are likely to forget that His blessings were indeed an answer to prayer—this, I believe, is why novenas are so powerful.) Finally, we should note that discernment essentially amounts to hearing (and heeding) the voice of the Holy Spirit within us—but that quiet voice can be drowned out by three things which will destroy discernment: undisciplined flesh, worldly attachments, and constant noise.

Constant Prayer and a Preference for Silence. "Rejoice always, pray constantly, give thanks in all circumstances; for this is the will of God in Christ Jesus for you." (I Thessalonians 5:16-18) Scripture, we see, admonishes us to pray not sometimes, not often, and not *almost* always… but rather, it tells us to pray *constantly*. Instead of seeing this as a burden, however, we should see this as a joy. The Almighty Creator of the Universe desires to always be in conversation with you! And if we acquiesce to this loving desire of His, the Gift is ours. It is that simple. Jesus tells Luisa that He simply cannot resist a soul that undertakes a continuous effort to converse with Him (cf. July 28, 1902).

Abnegation. With the virtue of abnegation, we let go of everything but God Himself, and we especially let go that which is closest and dearest to us: our own will. Jesus did not fail to model this virtue for us: **"Thy Will, not mine, be done."** (Luke 22:42) If those blessed words of our Blessed Lord are always on our lips, and if we simply try to mean them more and more each time we say them, then we are well on our way to living the total abnegation—the total surrender—that Jesus wishes of us in order to live in His Will, and the Gift will be ours. And what a joyful occasion it is to so surrender; for God has a much better plan in His mind (even for our sanctity itself) than we ourselves could ever conjure up. Nevertheless, so many people want a "clearer" path to the goal of sanctity than the Will of God. So many want something more "tangible." Indeed, there are many clear and tangible *helps* to arrive at the end of sanctity; but not one of them is sanctity itself. And what happens if we cast this truth aside? We fall directly into the devil's snares:

> The thing which [the devil] abhors the most is that the creature do my Will. He does not care whether the soul prays, goes to Confession, goes to Communion, does penance or makes miracles; but the thing which harms him the most is that the soul do my Will, because as he rebelled against my Will, then was hell created in him…(September 9, 1923)

While never detracting from the many important means to the end of sanctity, we must remember that in God's Will, *and in God's Will alone,* is where sanctity is found. The Will of God is already perfectly simple, and therefore it cannot be reduced to anything simpler. And while it may at first be painful to hear that none of those exceedingly *holy things* can guarantee *your holiness* (but that only the Will of God can), this truth should in fact do nothing but allow a great peace to permeate your entire soul: for the Will of God is pure love, and it is always with you. It is never inaccessible; nothing can separate you from it. Through no fault of your own, you may be deprived of the Eucharist, Confession, the ability to perform works of mercy, etc. But no matter what has transpired thus far with respect to these things, the greatest sanctity is nevertheless knocking at your door this very moment, and always will be—all you need to do is say "yes" to it. *Fiat.* **Give everything—*everything*—to God. He will not be outdone in generosity. In fact, you will be inundated with a peace so perfect that none of your prior efforts ever succeeded in giving so much as a morsel of it.** So, let us turn now to Peace as a Foundational Virtue.

Perennial Peace and Trust. Mirroring perfectly what He had said earlier to Luisa, Jesus tells St. Faustina: "the greatest obstacles to holiness are discouragement and an exaggerated anxiety. These will deprive you of the ability to practice virtue." (§1488) Sin, therefore, is not the greatest obstacle to holiness; if it were, then we would be insane to do anything but find a remote monastery (utterly devoid of any occasion of sin) and join it. That is indeed a great calling, but it is not the genuine calling of most. In Luisa's letters, what she perhaps exhorted their recipients to most frequently was peace. Luisa knew that the constant temptation in our lives is to deprive ourselves of peace as if this were somehow called for, when in fact this deprivation is always an affront to the goodness of God, Who never desires that we be without peace. God wants to pour His grace into our lives; we prevent Him by preferring anxiety, worry, and fretfulness to peace and trust. Jesus tells Luisa:

> Distrust blocks the development of virtues, and puts freezing cold into the most ardent love. Oh! how many times, because of lack of trust, my designs and the greatest sanctities are blocked. This is why **I tolerate some defects rather than distrust—because those can never be so harmful**. (September 2, 1924) One of the purest joys that the creature can give Me is trust in Me. I feel her as My daughter, and I do what I want with her. I can say that trust makes Me known for who I am-that I am the Immense Being; My Goodness, without end; My Mercy, without limits. (May 26, 1935)

We should also have peace by reminding ourselves how glorious the Gift is—how many astounding promises come with It—and by recognizing how very easy It is to receive. Jesus tells Luisa: **"See then, how easy it is to live in Our Will: the creature does not have to do new things, but whatever she does—that is, to carry out her life as we gave it to her, in Our Will."** (May 17, 1938) And although Luisa knew that this Gift was and is the greatest sanctity of all, she never hesitated to insist that It was for all people; not just for religious, or priests, or the consecrated. In her letters, she wrote:

> Do you see, then, how easy it is? Nor does one have to be a religious to do this. The Sanctity of living in the Divine Will is for all; or rather, to tell the truth, It is for all those who want It. (Letter 19 to Mrs. Savorani) It takes nothing but a firm decision of wanting to live in the Holy Will. It is Jesus who wants it... [He] will reach the extent of making up for us in all that we are unable to do. (Letter 74 to Mrs. Valentino)

Courage and Fearlessness. Along with peace, one of the most prevalent exhortations found in all of Luisa's revelations is Jesus' admonition to the virtue of courage. When God has such great plans at work—and there is no greater plan than this mission of the Divine Will—timidity, fear, and lukewarmness destroy everything. Jesus tells Luisa:

> My daughter, timidity represses Grace and hampers the soul. A timid soul ... always has her eyes fixed on herself, and on the effort she makes in order to walk. Timidity makes her keep her eyes low, never high...On the other hand, **in one day a courageous soul does more than a timid one does in one year**. (February 12, 1908) ... **sloth produces many evils, physical and moral**...And then some dare to say that to these I give grace for them to make themselves saints, and to others I do not, almost wanting to hold Me responsible, while they content themselves with conducting their lives lazing about, as if the light of grace were not there for them. (October 20, 1916)

Courage will allow us to respond with zeal to the invitations God gives us instead of, as Jesus laments here, "lazing about." Courage, like charity, is not a feeling; it is certainly not a sensation which we are miraculously given before we set ourselves to work. Rather, it is a grace which emboldens our steps when they are made in accord with God's Will. Do not, therefore, sit idly wondering why you lack the courage to do God's Will; simply do God's Will, and trust that you will have the courage to persevere in It—and, as Jesus assures you, you will do so, saying:

> Only in the act in which the creature sets herself to do what I want, then am I drawn to give her the strength necessary, or rather, superabundant—not before ... **How many, before doing an action, feel so helpless, but as soon as they set to work they feel invested by new strength, by new light. I am the One who invests them, as I never fail in providing the necessary strength** that is needed in order to do some good. (May 15, 1938) Who acquires a name, nobility, heroism?—a soldier who sacrifices himself, who exposes himself in battle, who lays down his life for love of the king, or another who stands arms akimbo? Certainly the first one. (October 29, 1907)

While courage does not consist in the absence of the *feeling* of fear, it does require the absence of deliberately *willed* fear. So, let us turn to consider the general question of fear.

No Fear of Anything. Fear is not okay. It is always a temptation, and we ought never succumb to it. Jesus tells Luisa, "**My Will excludes *every* fear** ... Therefore, banish *every* fear, if you do not want to displease Me." (July 29, 1924) Those who are tempted to protest, "But didn't even Jesus fear the pains of His passion during the Agony in the Garden?" are in for quite a surprise in reading the upcoming section on the *Hours of the Passion*. "Well and good," another might say, "I shall be careful not to justify fearing pain, difficulty, and the like. But ought I not at least fear the devil?" *Certainly not*. Do not misunderstand: we must indeed zealously oppose the devil, despise him, and recognize that, as Scripture says, he "prowls around like a roaring lion, seeking someone to devour."(I Peter 5:8)[18] This does not mean, however, that we should fear him. His power, though enormous, is restrained by an infinitely greater one: that of God Himself who chained the devil with His own sacrifice on the cross. And *through this power of God*, the devil is no match for the soul who does not stray within the radius of that chain (through mortal sin, dabbling in the occult, flirtation with heresy, etc.). Jesus tells Luisa:

> Daughter, temptations can be conquered easily, because **the devil is the most cowardly creature that can exist**, and a contrary act, a contempt, a prayer, are enough to make him flee. ... as soon as he sees the soul resolute in not wanting to pay attention to his cowardice, he flees terrified. (March 25, 1908)

But what about death itself? Shall we fear that? *Absolutely not.* Jesus speaks the most consoling words imaginable to Luisa about the moment of death; so much so that anyone who realizes that these words are genuinely from Our Lord will, upon reading them, lose all fear of that moment. Jesus tells Luisa:

> [At the moment of death,] the walls fall down, and she can see with her own eyes what they had told her before. She sees her God and Father, Who has loved her with great love. One by one, she sees the benefits that He has done to her, and how she has broken all the rights of love that she owed Him. She sees how her life belonged to God, not to herself. ...My Goodness is such, wanting everyone to be saved, that I allow the falling of these walls when the creatures find themselves between life and death—at the moment in which the soul exits the body to enter eternity—so that they may make at least one act of contrition and of love for Me, recognizing my adorable Will over them. I can say that I give them one hour of truth, in order to rescue them. **Oh! if all knew my industries of love, which I perform in the last moment of their lives,** so that they might not escape from my hands, more than paternal—

they would not wait for that moment, but they would love Me all their lives. (March 22, 1938)

What about fearing Jesus? *Above all* we must not fear Him! Do not be scandalized: we ought never slacken in our *Holy* **Fear** (the filial fear that is a genuine gift of the Holy Spirit and can also be described as awe), nor may we ever let our reverence fade. But we also must never forget that perfect love casts out all fear (cf. I John 4:18) and Living in the Divine Will requires perfect love. Now, I am speaking here of servile fear: the fear of punishment. This is the type of fear that must be cast out by perfect love. He tells Luisa:

> **I feel sad when they think that I am severe**, and that I make more use of Justice than of Mercy. They act with Me as if I were to strike them at each circumstance. Oh! how dishonored I feel by these ones. … by just taking a look at my life, they can but notice that I did only one act of Justice—when, in order to defend the house of my Father, I took the ropes and snapped them to the right and to the left, to drive out the profaners. Everything else, then, was all Mercy: **Mercy my conception, my birth, my words, my works, my steps, the Blood I shed, my pains—everything in Me was merciful love**. Yet, they fear Me, while they should fear themselves more than Me. (June 9, 1922)

How could you fear Him? He has been closer to you than your mother, closer to you than your spouse—for your entire life—and, for the rest of your life, He will remain closer to you than anyone, until the moment your body is called forth from the depths of the earth at the General Judgment. **Nothing can separate you from the love of God. Do not fear Him.** Jesus also says to Luisa:

> As soon as a baby is conceived, My Conception goes around the conception of the baby, to form him and keep him defended. And as he is born, My Birth places itself around the newborn, to go around him and give him the helps of My Birth, of My tears, of My wailings; and even My Breath goes around him to warm him. **The newborn does not love Me, though unconsciously, and I Love him to folly;** I Love his innocence, My Image in him, I Love what he must be. My Steps go around his first vacillating steps in order to strengthen them, and they continue to go around unto the last step of his life, to keep his steps safe within the round of My Steps … And I can say that even My Resurrection goes around his sepulcher, waiting for the propitious time in order to call, by the Empire of My Resurrection, his Resurrection of the body to Immortal Life. (March 6, 1932)

Love of the Cross. In one entry in Luisa's diary, we read a revelation from a soul in Purgatory:

> **It takes nothing to know whether you are doing well or badly: if you appreciate suffering, you are doing well; if you don't, you are doing badly.** In fact, one who appreciates suffering, appreciates God; and by appreciating Him, one can never displease Him. … [Jesus adds:] My daughter, in almost all of the events that occur, creatures keep repeating, over and over again: 'And why? And why? And why? Why this illness? Why this interior state? Why this scourge?' And many other why's. The explanation of 'why' is not written on earth, but in Heaven, and there everyone will read it. Do you know what 'why' is? It is egoism, which gives continuous food to love of self. Do you know where 'why' was created? In hell. Who was the first one that pronounced it? A demon. … And do you know where 'why' will be buried? In hell, to make them restless for eternity, without ever giving them peace. The art of 'why' is to wage war against souls, without ever giving them respite. (January 30, 1909)

By repudiating the "why," Jesus is of course not condemning inquiry into matters deserving investigation; He is, rather, insisting that we not ask the accusatory "why" every time something goes the way our self-wills did not want it to go. We must instead understand that, as St. Alphonsus Liguori said, "**it is certain and of faith that, whatever happens, happens by the Will of God.**" Yes, it really **is** that simple. If it happened, it was God's Will; whether it transpired by virtue of His *wanted* Will or His *permissive* Will makes no difference as far as our submission is concerned. By grumbling about what has happened, we lament God's Will. How are we supposed to submit to—much less *live in*—God's Will if we lament that very thing? Complaining of any sort has no place in the life of any Christian and should be especially repudiated by one who wishes to live in the Divine Will. But we must go farther than merely refuse to complain of crosses; we must *love* them. And how can we love the cross? If a cross is by definition that which we suffer in receiving, and if suffering is needing to endure that which we do not want, then is this not a fundamental contradiction? No, it is not a contradiction. "Folly to the gentiles," (I Corinthians 1:23) indeed, but not a contradiction. And it is none other than the Passion of the Christ, which He willingly and lovingly suffered for you, that enables this "folly of love" within your own heart. Let His Passion be always before you, and you will then love the cross just as Our Lord loved His own for your sake. Specifically, in this regard, we ought to often do the *Hours of the Passion*, which is discussed in a forthcoming section.

Constancy. Remember that Jesus is asking that we be like Him in everything. And Jesus, as God, never changed. One of the clearest proofs that an individual is devoid of grace—and, certainly, does not live in God—is a moody, unstable demeanor, or having tastes, intentions, and goals that are constantly changing. Sometimes giddy, other times depressed and irritable. Sometimes on fire for the salvation souls, sometimes caring only for vain, worldly hobbies. Jesus tells Luisa:

> **The soul who is not completely mine is empty**... she is in a continuous alternation of tastes and disgusts; and since any taste which did not come from Me is not lasting, many times tastes turn into disgusts, and this is why many variations of character can be noticed: **now too sad, now too cheerful, now all irascible, another time all affable. It is the void of Me which she has in her soul that gives her so many variations of character.** (June 6, 1923) My daughter, **one who really loves Me never gets annoyed about anything**, but tries to convert all things into love. (July 22, 1905)

✳✳✳

At this point, no doubt, I have given you plenty of virtues to work on! But now that you have your "background" work cut out for you (not, of course, that virtue is less important than what follows—but virtue comes largely as a consequence of *moving*, as we said in this section's beginning), let us now turn our attention to our *forefront* work: our mission.

Proclaim the Kingdom

Now that you know some of these most sublime truths of the Divine Will, it is imperative that you not keep them to yourself! **To Luisa, Jesus likens those who spread knowledge of this Third Fiat to the very Evangelists who wrote the Gospels.** (cf. January 18, 1928) **There are even ways in which our duty is more exciting and privileged; what they longed for; we are now on the cusp of attaining. At what time it is attained, and who shares in its attainment, is dependent upon our response—that is, the response of the relative few reading these words.**

What sacrifice, then, is too great to spread this Kingdom of His on earth? What vanity, now clung to, is not worth casting aside for the sake of the Reign of His Will? What risk, now feared, is not worth taking to be able to participate in the initiation of the Third Fiat of the Eternal One? Patriarchs, Prophets, Martyrs, Fathers, Doctors, and yes, even the Angels, envy you for the invitation that God extends freely to you. Take it.

> If creatures possessed my Divine Will as life, they would know many beautiful things about It; and knowing It and **not speaking about It would be impossible for them**; therefore they would do nothing else but speak of It, love It and lay down their lives in order not to lose It. (January 16, 1930) Therefore, my daughter, my goodness is so great that **I reward justly and superabundantly the good that the creature does, especially in this work of my Will, which I so much care for.** What will I not give to those who occupy and sacrifice themselves in order to place in safety the rights of my Eternal Fiat? I will exceed so much in giving, as to make Heaven and earth astonished. (February 28, 1928)

Jesus will give so much to you if you work to live in and promote the Divine Will, that He will astonish Heaven and earth in this giving. Elsewhere, He says that if only we had the faintest clue of what He has prepared for us, then those of us who know about these revelations to Luisa on His Will would "lay down their lives in order to fling [these truths] into the midst of the world." (August 26, 1928) *He needs your effort now* so that you can lay the necessary groundwork before the Reign of His Will can commence:

> Although I burn with the desire of seeing My Divine Will Reign, yet I cannot give this Gift before I have manifested the Truths…So, giving the great Gift of My Divine Will-which more than sun will change the lot of the human generations-today, would be to give It to the blind. And giving It to the blind would be giving them useless gifts, and I do not know how to give useless things. Therefore, **I await with Divine and delirious patience that My Truths will make their way…More than father We yearn to give the Great Gift of Our Will to Our children, but We want that they know what they are receiving…**(May 15, 1932) [These knowledges serve as] powerful reproaches to those who should occupy themselves with making known a Good so Great, and who, out of indolence and vain fears, will not let them go around through the whole world, so that they may bring the Good News of the Happy Era of the Kingdom of My Will. (January 24, 1932)

But who are "those who should occupy themselves"? *Whoever has read these words—* Jesus' words to Luisa—which have been read by such a minuscule percentage of the world. That is, *you!* **You are utterly precious and pivotal in God's plan by the mere fact that you have been exposed to this.** In "stumbling upon" you through your reading of these words, God is more fortunate than is a beggar who has stumbled upon a millionaire willing to part with his fortunes. For God has found in you someone who can help hasten His greatest plan: that His Will be done on earth as it is done in Heaven. So, what can you do? *Just get the truth out there:* succinctly, charitably, and poignantly, however you possibly can. There is no use in me instructing you on the details of how to do that. You know how you can do your part to cause these revelations to explode into the world: do it. No excuses. Make it happen. Whatever it takes. Rest when you die, not now. Proclaim the Kingdom. Be a New Evangelist of the Third Fiat. **"And Jesus said to him: Let the dead bury their dead: but go thou, and preach the kingdom of God."**–Luke 9:60

Jesus assures Luisa that the only thing needed for this Kingdom to come is souls willing to proclaim it: **"All that is needed are those who would offer themselves to be the criers**—and with courage, without fearing anything, facing sacrifices in order to make it known…"(August 25, 1929) Jesus already did the hard part with Luisa decades ago. All we need to do now is to pick the fruit of the tree over which she and He so labored. Furthermore, hastening the coming of the Kingdom is the most noble effort one can undertake; completely immune from the various ulterior motives that so often sneak into many other holy endeavors. Jesus tells Luisa that, in so doing:

> You seek nothing for yourself, and you go round and round, asking over and over again that My Divine Will be known, and that It dominate and reign. **Not a shadow of what is human enters into this, nor any personal interest; it is the holiest and most Divine prayer and act; it is prayer of Heaven**, not of the earth, and therefore the purest, the most beautiful, the invincible one, that encloses only the interest of the Divine Glory. (August 12, 1927)

We must show God that we want this Kingdom, so that His bestowal of it consists in His answering our ardent prayers. Jesus tells Luisa that, in this regard, He is not unlike a leader in this world, who wishes to do what he does in response to his people wanting it (cf. May 30, 1928). Know, too, that in hastening the coming of the Kingdom, you are entering into the most holy and joyous endeavor with the very saints in Heaven. Like good friends competing in a sport, you and they are both endeavoring zealously to see who can do more to hasten the arrival of this Reign on earth (for the souls in Heaven want this Reign even more than the souls on earth do; due to the latter often being subject to doubts and short-sightedness). (cf. May 20, 1928) And, of course, it is not only the ardent desire of the saints, but of Jesus Himself, Who tells Luisa:

> **If I prayed and cried and desired it was only for my kingdom that I wanted in the midst of creatures,** because He being the holiest thing, my Humanity could do no less (than) to want and to desire the holiest thing in order to sanctify the desires of everyone and give them that which was holy and of the greatest and perfect good for them. (January 29, 1928) **The first indispensable necessity** in order to obtain the Kingdom of the Divine **Will is to ask for It with Incessant prayers**... [the] **second necessity**, more indispensable than the first, in order to obtain this Kingdom: it is necessary **to know that one can have It**. ... If the Ancients had not known that the future Redeemer was to come, no one would have given it a thought ... When it is known that a Good can be possessed, arts and industriousness are used, and the means to obtain the intent are employed...The **third necessary means is to know that God wants to give this Kingdom.** (March 20, 1932)

Yes, God wants to give this Kingdom even more than we want to receive it. *It will come.* Banish every doubt, for these will sap you of the energy you need to hasten its coming. But even Luisa once expressed a doubt about the coming of the Kingdom, and we see the following exchange between Jesus and Luisa:

> [Luisa:] "But who knows who will see when this Kingdom of the Divine Fiat will come? O! how difficult it seems." ... [Jesus:] "My daughter, and yet It will come. You measure the human, the sad times that involve the present generations, and therefore it seems difficult to you. ... what is impossible for human nature, is easy for Us...And then, there is **the Queen of Heaven who, with Her Empire, continuously prays that the Kingdom of the Divine Will come on earth**, and when have We ever denied Her anything? For Us, Her Prayers are impetuous winds such that We cannot resist Her... **She will give Unheard-of Graces, Surprises never seen, Miracles that will shake Heaven and earth. We give Her the whole field free so that She will form for Us the Kingdom of Our Will on earth.** She will be the Guide, the True Model, It will also be the Kingdom of the Celestial Sovereign. Therefore, you also pray together with Her, and at Its time you will obtain the intent. (July 14, 1935)

Our Lady herself is begging her Divine Son for the coming of the Kingdom on earth. **We've already experienced some of Our Lady's miracles that have, as Jesus said, "shaken Heaven and earth," but we can rest assured that many more are coming soon.** Of course, there are those who denounce the Era and Our Lady's intercession, and they will not abandon their denunciation. But they cannot stop the Era. Jesus tells Luisa:

> When [the Divine Will] decides to operate in one creature in order to fulfill Its greatest designs in the midst of the human generations, It lets no one dictate to It the law—neither who it must be, nor the time, nor the way, nor the place—but It acts in an absolute way. Nor does It pay heed to **certain short minds, which are unable to elevate themselves in the divine and supernatural order, or to bow their forehead to the incomprehensible works of their Creator;** and while they want to reason with their own human reason, they lose the divine reason, and remain confounded and incredulous. (May 19, 1931)

Let Your Cry be Continuous

The present world is in many ways a rather miserable place; consequently, there are two kinds of people to be found within it. There are those who are continually irritated, annoyed, anxious, depressed, and even downright furious; and there are those who have found fleeting relief from such ailments by self-medicating with some psychological or physiological trick they play on themselves—engaging in self-deceit through the "Power of Positive Thinking," practicing self-harm with the abuse of legal or illegal substances, or dedicating themselves with unbounded effort to some vain ambition whose fleeting rewards will scarcely be noticed moments after they have begun.

But, actually, there is a third group of people, and I invite you to join its ranks. These people are honest about the sorry state of the world as it plays out in the details of their own trials, in the grand paradigm-shifts of geopolitics, and in everything in-between; they do not pretend these ills are anything other than things to be justly lamented and striven against. Thus, they are as far from the second group described above as a lung doctor is from a cigarette salesman. Despite this honesty, however, they never descend to the antics of those in the first group; for each and every time they are confronted with the sorry state of the world in any of its diverse incarnations, they approach such situations precisely in accordance with what they are: invitations and reminders to engage in battle against the prince of this world—the devil—by imploring God for the coming of the Kingdom, wherein all such sorry things will scarcely be a memory. Far as they are from the second group, it is equally true that they are as far from the first group as a U.S. Marine is from an opinionated armchair Twitter activist. One basks in the glory of victory even while still engaged in battle; the other only rants and grows ever more plagued with anxiety.

Remain continually in this third group, and you *will* succeed in calling down the Kingdom of God upon earth. Has there been another mass shooting? Or just another tantrum thrown by your 2-year-old? Always respond—interiorly, at least— *"Lord, let Your Kingdom come."* Terrorists on the rampage, massacring innocent civilians in Africa? Or just obnoxious neighbors at it again with their music, arguing, and revving engines? The nations appear to be preparing for World War III? Or is it discord within your marriage, family, or friends? Thousands of acres of God's Creation destroyed by a nuclear meltdown? Or, is just the ugliness of litter, billboards, and hideous buildings presented before your eyes? Are you dreading some great looming trial in your life—a major surgery, an impending death of a loved one; or, are you just feeling subjected to various depressions and anxieties that come with your ordinary life's endeavors? **Respond to all these situations the same way, and never neglect to do so, that your cry may be continuous:** *"Lord, let your Kingdom come!"*

Are you in the midst of any personal suffering—great or small? Say always: "Jesus, I Trust in You. Thy Will be Done. I offer this suffering to You for the coming of Your Kingdom." Or, are you blessed to have no particular lamentable thing presenting itself to you in the moment? Then simply pray incessantly—so repeatedly that God Himself cannot bear hearing it from you anymore without granting it—the greatest petition of the greatest prayer ever uttered by the lips of man:

Thy Will be done on earth as it is in Heaven, Thy Will be done on earth as it is in Heaven, Thy Will be done on earth as it is in Heaven.

Of course, this continuous cry ought not be restricted to times when a response is needed to evils you observe. I merely present such situations as one category of reminders to cry out for the Kingdom. We should harbor equal zeal in crying out for the Kingdom whenever we witness anything good, true, or beautiful—for in such cases, we are pleading for the universal reign of these noble things we witness. What strikes you each day? A beautiful sunset? The glory of a small flower? The love of family and good friends? The chirping of the birds? All such things are invitations from God to thank Him, bless Him, glorify Him, and beg Him for the coming of His Kingdom, wherein His goodness, truth, and beauty shall reign supreme on earth—universally and without interruption. As Jesus implores Luisa and us all, **"Therefore, you—pray, and let your cry be continuous: 'May the Kingdom of your Fiat come, and your Will be done on earth as It is in Heaven.'"** (May 31, 1935)

Another dimension of our continuous cry for the Kingdom is the need to impress everything with our own *Fiat*. What has happened, has happened; what will happen, will happen—all because Almighty God deliberately has chosen or will choose to inspire it or at least allow it—therefore, we can glorify His Will in all these things and thereby contribute to our own eternal glory and the coming of the Kingdom; or we can complain, and thereby detract from the same. Accordingly, consider: what now tempts you to dwell on regret? An opportunity for more money, recognition, worldly memories, possessions, security, travels, comfort, pleasure—or whatever other vanity—having sailed on by? A loved one having died, and what seems to be a lost future with him? Forgiven sins coming to mind to haunt you and tempt you to despair because of their mere existence? Submit to the Will of God in all these things—for, with the Gift, all of these apparent losses are absolutely nothing at all—say to Him, about such things whenever they come to mind, "Lord, I offer you my Fiat; let Your Holy Will be glorified, loved, and adored. I thank You and I bless You in all Your works," and every apparent loss you have ever suffered or will ever suffer is transfigured into a thing of immeasurable eternal glory and constitutes another call for the Kingdom to come upon earth. As Jesus tells Luisa, "The more [the soul] is deprived of tastes, pleasures, amusements, trips, strolls on earth, the more tastes and pleasures she will have in God ... one who leaves the earth, takes Heaven, be it even in the smallest thing." (September 7, 1908)

Till the Soil

The Kingdom will come on earth as a miraculous, unprecedented, and overwhelming Divine Intervention, in response to our ardent prayers for precisely that; hence the erroneous nature of Liberation Theology, Utopianism, Secular Messianism, Progressive Evolutionism, some forms of Marxism, and similar false ideologies, each of which—in its own way—supposes that a future golden age may arrive on earth *as a consequence of human effort,* or as a mere automatic unfolding of events already in progress. (Millenarianism, on the other hand, is a distinct error, and it is addressed in this book's appendices.)

But it does not follow from the erroneous nature of these -isms that those who rightly await the *genuine* Era are exempt from doing their part to physically aid its coming! As Padre Pio said, "work as if everything depended upon you, pray as if everything depended upon God." Ever cognizant that our efforts will not be the *cause* of the Era, we who long for God's Kingdom on earth should nevertheless be very zealous in working to promote and incarnate those very goods that will flourish abundantly during its Reign, lest we fall into the opposite errors of those listed above (e.g. Quietism, Providentialism, or even simple apathy). Similarly, no gardener pretends that his own tilling of the soil is what causes the growth of the plants therein, but this does not inhibit his diligence in so doing. We, too, who await and pray for the Era, should be sure we do not slacken in our evangelization and proclamation of the Divine Mercy, our working for justice and the common good, our fighting for the truth, our insistence upon and promotion of beauty, our involvement in politics, etc.; in a word, our doing all that we can to ensure that when Christ comes in grace to reign as King during the Era, He already as much as possible finds Himself socially reigning as King through the fruits of our labors even now. In Jesus' revelations to Luisa, we see anything but a God disinterested in such matters. Quite the contrary, Jesus tells Luisa to intercede for those who fight for what is good and true in the world—even in politics. Furthermore, as we will see in Chapter 4, Chastisements *will* precede the Era. These Chastisements will be mitigated most especially by our imploring the Divine Mercy and promoting the Divine Will; but they will also be mitigated by our own labors to accomplish through reform what otherwise will need to be accomplished through suffering.

Here, I will briefly share some of my own endeavors in tilling the soil in case anyone wishes to receive instruction or inspiration from my efforts or, perhaps, even join me in undertaking them. Above all, our duty in tilling is to evangelize. Redemption—and the Gospel that proclaims it—is the ultimate preparation for the Kingdom. The essence of this Gospel, the Divine Mercy, must therefore be now preached more zealously than ever. This task, however, is ill-suited to mere apologetics; people need to see witnesses, which I hope is found in the Divine Will Missionaries of Mercy (www.DWMoM.org). I have also put together a website aimed solely at evangelizing anyone who stumbles upon it, no matter where he is coming from (www.PrepareToSeeHim.org). With this site, I attempted to answer the question: "If Our Lady came, not in an apparition, but in a website, what would that website look like?" We must also be on fire for the truth, and in my capacity as a philosopher, I seek to promote and defend it (www.DOCPhilosophy.com). Politics remains one of the most powerful ways to quickly enact change for the better, and despite how corrupt those within politics often become, we must not "throw out the baby with the bathwater," but, instead, we must promote the Common Good through it (www.CommonGoodPlatform.com). Of all the issues that politics deals with, it is difficult to think of one more urgent than the right to life—from natural conception to natural death. Although I personally have not started an apostolate in this regard, I encourage all to consider participating in 40 Days for Life campaigns or anything similar. Finally, we ought not neglect doing what we are called to even when it comes to the physical aspects of making this world a better place; I pursue this goal with my efforts to develop inventions that could help those on this earth who are most in physical need (www.SJMechanicalSolutions.com). **But, as we all have vastly different callings in how to go about tilling the soil, I will now leave you with a general exhortation to be zealous instead of listing even more specific endeavors in which to engage. Listen to God and He will tell you how He wishes you to accomplish your part.** *Do not bury your talents.* Jesus has made it clear that neither "but I was tired," nor "but I was afraid," will work as excuses on the Day of Judgment. (cf. Matthew 25:14-30)

A final note on tilling the soil: when I speak of this, I am referring to those *external* actions in which we engage in order to better conform the temporal order to the Will of God. Notwithstanding the genuine importance of such endeavors (which I pray this section's final paragraph in no way diminishes), what far outshines them is that which is undertaken in a hidden and internal way—those deeds done between the soul and God. On the Day of Judgment it will be revealed that those who achieved the most to save and sanctify souls and usher in the Kingdom were not the great men whose biographies we all know, but those hidden and forgotten ones who always operated in union with God: monks and nuns in monasteries living lives of prayer and sacrifice without ever being thanked, patients suffering in hospitals and nursing homes and offering it all to Christ, ordinary parishioners spending many hours in Eucharistic adoration, humble housewives and menial laborers who do all that they do with love and in the Divine Will. Till the soil, indeed, dear reader: but do not become a mere activist who neglects what is internal and hidden for the sake of what is external and recognized by men, for that would be like a soldier snubbing a sword for the sake of a child's toy. Your most powerful weapons will always be those that are immune from the risk of self-interest and vanity.

Grow in the Knowledges

Not in vain did Jesus give Luisa thousands of pages of utterly astounding revelations! Nor did He do so merely that some author might come along one day and write a 100-page book summarizing them to dispense all from reading the revelations themselves. No, He revealed these truths to Luisa because He wants them known, read, and understood by all! What I have presented to you within the pages of this small book is no *substitute for* Luisa's revelations—it is an *invitation into* them! (My larger book, *The Crown of Sanctity*, is also only an invitation into the same.)

It is impossible for me to here state how glorious learning even one additional truth about the Divine Will is. **Jesus promises that each new truth you learn about His Will as revealed to Luisa gives you more strength to live in the Divine Will, embellishes your eternal home in Heaven, causes all the saints to rejoice, and hastens the coming of the Kingdom.** All these promises and so many more like them go with *merely coming to know* a single new truth about the Divine Will! Nowhere else will you find a few seconds of your time so generously rewarded. Try to have Luisa's writings always handy and read them regularly (I also highly recommend having an audiobook of them for listening to while driving, doing manual labor, etc.). **"See then, what it means to know one truth more, or one truth less—if all knew what great goods they miss, they would compete in order to acquire truths."** (Jesus to Luisa, January 25, 1922) These promises need not merely be taken on Faith, for the graces are *palpable*. If you are in God's grace and open Luisa's revelations with the sincere desire to learn the truths within them, you will *feel* yourself being inundated with new graces each time you read (or re-read!). Don't just take my word for it; see for yourself. And do not forget that these knowledges will cause the Kingdom of God to come upon earth:

> **The knowledges will be the messengers, the heralds, which will announce my Kingdom...They will form the true renewal of the world**...when creatures, conquered by the knowledges of my Divine Will, will say: 'You have won—we are now prey to your Kingdom.' (October 30, 1927)

Do the Hours of the Passion

Beyond her 36 Volumes, two works of Luisa's stand out: the *Blessed Virgin Mary in the Kingdom of the Divine Will* (which we will consider in the next section), and the object of our present consideration—the *Hours of the Passion*—a short work in which we mystically follow, hour by hour, Jesus and Mary through all the events of the Passion. We start with Jesus departing from His Blessed Mother before the Last Supper, and proceed all the way to the same Holy Mother departing the tomb after her Son's Sacred Body was laid inside it. Recall that Pope St. Pius X himself, when presented with these *Hours* by St. Hannibal, said that they should be read "while kneeling," because "it is Jesus Christ who is speaking" in them. The intuition of this holy Pope will be vindicated by your own when you dive into this most astounding revelation.

In reading, praying, and meditating upon these *Hours*, we act as victim souls, mystically suffer redemptively with Jesus, and foster our desire to give over our whole lives to Him. Indeed, in the *Hours of the Passion* we do far more than simply recall; we enter, rather, into each moment through the same bilocation of our souls that is made possible by the Gift. We fuse each of our members with Jesus', kissing Him as we strive to endure His passion with Him, thus offering Him consolation and assuming the role of quasi-co-redemptrix along with Our Lady, the true Co-Redemptrix. Jesus gave enormous promises to Luisa with these *Hours*, promises that extend to whoever undertakes them. He promised that through them, the saint would become holier still, the tempted would find victory, the ill would find strength, and that, **for each word read, the salvation of a soul would be granted.** He said that an entire city could be spared chastisements if only one soul in it would continually pray these *Hours*. **For the next few pages, therefore, I wish only to give you a taste of these *Hours* in hopes that you will be inspired to secure a copy for yourself and dive in head-first.**

What has always stayed with me from the *Hours* is that Jesus' words in the garden, "If it be possible, let this chalice pass" (Matthew 26:39) were not at all regarding apprehension of physical sufferings. Unspeakably dreadful as the physical sufferings were, Jesus was about as afraid of them as you would be afraid of getting wet to go and rescue your drowning child from a pool. These words of His referred, rather, to souls that, despite His love, would choose to condemn themselves to hell. For Jesus knew it was possible for the Father to exercise such dominion that He could simply override even the most perverse soul in order to force it into Heaven. But this would contradict the greatest gift with which God endowed the soul's substance—its free will. Therefore, in the ultimate act of submission to the Divine Will and as a model for us all, Jesus appended His petition with "nevertheless not My Will, but Thine be done," even knowing what He was about to suffer beyond any measure for them. That is the extent of His love; that blood would burst forth from His pores in agony over the loss of His children. It was the damnation of souls that caused Him to sweat blood, and to undergo His most horrible passion there in the garden. Any suffering the soldiers could hope to inflict upon Him with their devices of torture amounted to nothing close; the external passion and pain was absolutely nothing compared to the internal passion and sorrow as He took upon Himself all the evil that had ever been done or would ever be done. He truly desired to empty out every drop of His blood, to offer every square inch of His flesh for laceration, and to feel every imaginable pain. His burning love knew no bounds, and the more He suffered, the more superabundant grace He won for His beloved creatures.

Because of this, **we see throughout His passion Jesus actually burning with desire to suffer more and more. This desire was not like that of some crazed man infatuated with pain, but as one so unspeakably inflamed with love that nothing—not even the greatest sufferings imaginable—could stand in His way of doing everything possible for His children:**

> In order to form the Redemption, one Tear of Mine, one Sigh, was enough, but My Love would not have remained content. Being able to give and to do even more, My Love would have remained blocked in itself, and would not have been able to boast by saying: 'I have done everything, I have suffered everything, I have given you everything.' (April 16, 1933)

This love welled up as a consuming fire within Him that caused more suffering than the Passion itself, in its superabundance and in its need to expend and pour out itself entirely. And whenever His soul cried out in sorrow, it was not due to the internal or external pain, but due to seeing souls—past, present, and future—utterly refusing Him, hating Him, and choosing hell simply to spurn Him. In the *Hours* we read that He saw these souls as He looked down upon chunks of His own flesh torn off by the scourging, and it was that sight that caused Him in anguish to cry out. We read that at the height of agony, at His abandonment upon the cross, He entered into a conversation with these souls begging them not to choose hell, **begging them to go so far as to let Him suffer more and more if only they would permit Him to save them.**

Nowhere else will you come across so brutal a description of His passion as you will in Luisa's *Hours of the Passion*, and yet you will not come across a truer and more accurate one, either. Throughout these *Hours*, you will say, along with Luisa, and with the angels and saints, *"Is such great love possible?"* It is possible—not for man, but for God. And in Jesus, it is a reality.

If you have seen Mel Gibson's *The Passion of the Christ*, then you have a small idea of the brutality of the scourging at the pillar. But Jesus reveals more about it to Luisa than even that powerful movie shows (all the following quotes in this section are taken from the corresponding Hour in *The Hours of the Passion*):

> At the first blows, that flesh, beaten and wounded, rips open even more, and falls to the ground, torn into pieces. The bones are uncovered, the Blood pours down—so much, as to form a pool of Blood around the pillar... You say: "All of you who love Me, come to learn the heroism of true love! Come to dampen in my Blood the thirst of your passions, your thirst for so many ambitions... [Jesus converses with the Father during His scourging:] My Father, may each blow of these scourges repair before You for each kind of sin—one by one. **And as they strike Me, let them justify those who commit them. May these blows strike the hearts of creatures, and speak to them about my love, to the point of forcing them to surrender to Me."**
> And as You say this, your love is so great, though great is the pain, that You almost incite the executioners to beat You more. ... Your love is not tired, while the executioners are exhausted

and cannot continue your painful massacre. They now cut the ropes, and You, almost dead, fall into your own Blood. And in seeing the shreds of your flesh, You feel like dying of grief, because in those detached pieces of flesh You see the reprobate souls. And your sorrow is such, that You gasp in your own Blood...My Jesus, infinite Love, the more I look at You, the more I comprehend how much You suffer. You are already completely lacerated—there is not one point left whole in You.

Despite the so many atrocities that followed—the condemnations, the crowning with thorns, the continued tortures inflicted by the soldiers—the unbelievable love here displayed was not dimmed one iota, but only grew ever more inflamed. **Even while hanging upon the cross, He continued to beg for souls and to plea for more sufferings by virtue of which He won their salvation:**

[Upon the cross, in the moment of abandonment,] after so much suffering, with immense sorrow You see that not all souls are incorporated in You. Rather, You see that many will be lost, and You feel the painful separation of them, as they detach themselves from your limbs. And You, having to satisfy Divine Justice also for them, feel the death of each one of them, and the very pains they will suffer in hell. And You cry out loudly, to all hearts: "Do not abandon Me. If you want more pains, I am ready—but do not separate yourselves from my Humanity. ... everything else would be nothing, if I did not have to suffer your separation from Me! O please, have pity on my Blood, on my wounds, on my death! This cry will be continuous to your hearts. O please, do not abandon Me!" ... more than the abandonment of the Father, it is the loss of the souls who move far away from You that makes this painful lament escape from your Heart!

If it were not for the loss of souls, everything else—all the unheard-of tortures we have read about in the *Hours*—would be *nothing* for Jesus. **It is only for souls that He thirsts. We, dear readers, can quench that thirst of Jesus. Give Him your soul. Give Him your will. Tell souls about His unfathomable mercy. Admonish all to trust in His mercy. Remain ever close to Him in His suffering. Offer yourself completely to Him and love Him with all your heart.**

Immediately before His Holy Death, nature itself, horrified at the sight of its Creator so treated, prostrates before Jesus. And even His persecutors are reduced to silence, as something that no one present (except Our Lady) could have predicted transpires:

Horrified at such great crime, nature prostrates itself before You, and waits in silence for a word from You, to pay You honor and let your dominion be recognized. The sun, crying, withdraws its light, unable to sustain your sight, too sorrowful. Hell is terrified and waits in silence. Everything is silence. ... [the Jews present] and the ruthless executioners who, up to a little while ago, were offending You, mocking You, calling You impostor, criminal; even the thieves who were cursing You—everyone is silent, mute. Remorse invades them, and if they try to launch an insult against You, it dies on their lips. But ... I see that love overflows; it suffocates You and You cannot contain it. And forced by your love that torments You more than the pains themselves, with strong and moving voice, You speak as the God You are; You raise your dying eyes to Heaven, and exclaim: "Father, forgive them, for they know not what they are doing!" ... **Crucified Jesus, how can so much love be possible?** Ah, after so many pains and insults, your first word is of forgiveness; and You excuse us before the Father for so many sins! Ah, You make this word descend into each heart after sin, and You are the first to offer forgiveness. ... At this word, hell trembles and recognizes You as God; nature and everyone remain astonished; they recognize your Divinity, your inextinguishable love, and silently wait to see where it reaches. And not only your voice, but also your Blood and your wounds, cry out to every heart after sin: "Come into my arms, for I forgive you, and the seal of forgiveness is the price of my Blood." O my lovable Jesus, repeat this word again to all the sinners which are in the world. Beseech mercy for all; apply the infinite merits of your most precious Blood for all.

After His death, Jesus enters Limbo; bringing paradise to the countless souls there who have been waiting for Him for many centuries. But His Sacred Body still hung upon that cross, and Providence was not done using this Body as the Savior of mankind:

> And if your mouth is mute, your Heart speaks to me, and I hear It say: "My child, after I gave everything, I wanted this lance to open a shelter for all souls inside this Heart of Mine. Opened, It will cry out to all, continuously: Come into Me if you want to be saved. In this Heart you will find sanctity and you will make yourselves saints; you will find relief in afflictions, strength in weakness, peace in doubts, company in abandonments. O souls who love Me, if you really want to love Me, come to dwell in this Heart forever."

Dwell always in that Most Sacred Heart, pierced for love of you.

Listen to Your Heavenly Mother

As so many great saints—especially in recent times—have discovered, Mary is the key to sanctity; she is the key to her Son, and this is true as well with her Son's greatest Gift: His Divine Will. The last entry in all of Luisa's volumes is from December 28th, 1938. Although Luisa did not know it was to be the last, Jesus did, and He chose to dedicate it to His mother, saying:

> 'Mother of Mine, I want You to be the Mother of all, and what You have done for Me, You will do for all creatures'... the whole of Heaven prays and anxiously awaits the Divine Will to be known and to reign. Then will the Great Queen do to the children of my Will what She did for Her Jesus, and Her Maternity will have life in Her children. I will surrender my own place in Her Maternal Heart to those who live in my Will. She will raise them for Me, She will guide their steps, She will hide them within Her Maternity and Sanctity. Her Maternal Love and Her Sanctity will be seen, impressed in all their acts; they will be Her true children, who will look like Me in everything. **Oh! how I would love for everyone to know that if they want to live in my Will, they have a powerful Queen and Mother who will make up for whatever they lack.** She will raise them on Her maternal lap...

Have more beautiful, consoling, inspiring, and powerful words on Our Lady's motherhood ever been spoken? We see here in the clearest terms that Mary is the Mediatrix of All Grace, and that we can and will receive everything from her hands. Perhaps most succinctly summing up the many teachings that He gave to Luisa on His mother, Jesus says: "... [My mother **Mary**] **received the unique mission as the Mother of a God Son, and the office of Co-Redemptrix of mankind... all other creatures combined, both celestial and terrestrial, would never be able to equal Her.**" (May 1, 1925) This statement, of course, refers to *all* creatures past, present, and future—which includes even all those who would be given the Gift of Living in the Divine Will—never equaling Our Lady. Indeed, even with the Gift, we remain just little children of our Heavenly Queen Mother. Time and time again throughout Luisa's 36 volumes, we see Jesus glorifying His mother, insisting that she is the way to the Gift of His Will, and encouraging our love of and devotion to her.

Therefore, the Queen of Heaven was, and is, the terror of all hell. Now the infernal serpent feels over his head my immediate word spoken to him in Eden—my irrevocable condemnation that a woman would crush his head. Therefore he knows that, by his head being crushed, his kingdom on earth will be overturned, he will lose his prestige, and all the evil he did in Eden by means of a woman will be made up for by another woman... the Celestial Lady is the true Queen of the Kingdom of my Will. (May 19, 1931) **She wants Her children on earth in the Kingdom where She Lived.** She is not content that She has Her children in Heaven in the Kingdom of the Divine Will, but She wants them also on earth. She feels that **She has not completed the task given to Her by God as Mother and Queen. As long as the Divine Will does not Reign on earth in the midst of creatures, Her Mission is not finished.** (May 20, 1936)

Indeed, Our Lady's mission is not finished. With no less conviction, then, we can say with the Apostles themselves (as they said 2,000 years ago) that we have the Queen of All Creation in our midst who will ensure that the Will of her Son is done. Jesus continues on this same thread, describing why—among many other reasons, of course—it is that Our Lady desires for this Gift to Reign on earth:

> My daughter, the Queen of Heaven, in Her glory and greatness, is as though isolated...She is the isolated Queen; She does not have the cortege of other queens who surround Her and match Her in the glory and greatness that She possesses. ... the Celestial Mama wants, desires-awaits the Kingdom of the Divine Will upon earth. (January 18, 1928)

The Sovereign Queen of Heaven wishes to be surrounded by royalty similar to herself. This simple sentence conveys an essential understanding of the whole Divine Will message. For in it we see that no one can ever exceed or even have the same position as Mary—that will always be hers alone. But no one wants only to be surrounded by inferiors; they want equals. I here share only a few tiny pieces of the astounding revelations Jesus gives Luisa on His mother, as it is urgent for all to read them for themselves in Luisa's volumes, along with the *Hours* we considered in the previous section.

The Blessed Virgin Mary in the Kingdom of the Divine Will. In this book (see the appendices to find out how to obtain it), our Blessed Mother teaches us lessons on how to live continuously in the Divine Will. This is the real design for the Gift; not that It be a passing thing, but that It define our entire life without the exception of a single moment. While *The Hours of the Passion* cover a 24-hour period, these lessons consist of meditations for each day over the course of a month—namely, the month of May. Each day contains three lessons: one for morning, one for noon, and one for evening. Mary begins the book by promising Luisa that she will do whatever it takes to form her children in the Divine Will: even if she must go to every family, nation, religious community, etc. In order that we may have some small idea of what a tremendous privilege it is to hear these lessons, Our Lady says:

> Look at Me, dear child: thousands of Angels surround Me and, reverent, are all in waiting, to hear Me speak of that Divine Fiat whose fount I possess, more than anyone; I know Its admirable secrets, Its infinite joys, Its indescribable happiness and Its incalculable value.

Learn from Our Lady; follow Our Lady; love Our Lady; be ever consecrated to Our Lady, and you will surely live in the Divine Will.

Do All Your Acts in the Divine Will

Scripture directs us to *"Put on the Lord Jesus Christ"* (Romans 13:14), and with the Gift we can accomplish this in the truest possible sense. Just as importantly as asking for the Gift, we should always ask Jesus to do with us, through us, and *in* us whatever we are doing at the moment. This is God's plan with the Gift; not that It be passively enjoyed, but that It be employed as the very life principle of all our acts—which, previously merely human, now become divinized.

With the Gift, Jesus is inviting us to have the operation within His very own Self *always* **be our** *primary* **endeavor.** Jesus tells Luisa that He re-did each of our lives during His thirty years of hidden life on earth; these "redone" version of our lives remain suspended in God, awaiting our entrance into the Divine Will to claim their acts for our own by doing all that we do in His Will. How often do we pause to consider that the Gospel which speaks so beautifully of Our Lord only really details the final three years of His thirty-three-year life on earth? Not often enough! And yet, He could have easily simply come to earth miraculously as a fully-grown man and achieved all He needed to very quickly. But instead, He spent decades doing those things we all must do. And this was not in vain. Jesus reveals to Luisa:

> If I walked, I had the virtue of being able to go from one city to another without making use of My steps, but I wanted to walk in order to place My Love in every step so that in every step it would run... I worked with St. Joseph in order to procure the necessities of life, [but] it was Love that ran. They were Conquests and Triumphs that I made, because one Fiat was enough for Me to have everything at My Disposal. And making use of My Hands for a little profit, the Heavens were amazed; the Angels remained enraptured and mute in seeing Me abase Myself to the humblest actions of life. But My Love had its outlet, it filled, overflowed, in My Acts, and I was always the Divine Conqueror and Triumpher... In fact I gave course to the most humble and base things of life that were not necessary for Me, but I did in order to form as many distinct ways in order to let My Love run ... in order to make a Gift of them to those I Loved so much. (April 16, 1933)

Fr. Iannuzzi expounds upon this stunning reality in his Doctoral Dissertation. He writes:

> Jesus assumed a humanity like that of Adam and, within himself, enclosed a kingdom for each creature. This kingdom was made up of all the divine acts that all humans were to have accomplished if Adam had not sinned. These divine acts were formed within Jesus' humanity, whose human will took possession of the Divine Will and vice-versa... For **Jesus' divine acts were ordered to the divinization of human nature and to empowering souls to accomplish the same divine acts that he accomplished.** Indeed, from the time of man's creation, the divine acts that God had prepared for all souls, and that await their actualization, were already present to the Son of God and their number established. (3.1, 3.1.1.1)

Jesus tells Luisa that when we perform our ordinary acts in the Divine Will, we form suns that, though small in themselves, nevertheless succeed in investing all creation with the light and heat of their splendor; just as the sun, which appears small in relation to the sky it inhabits, gives its light and heat to all the earth. These suns are formed by Jesus truly doing in us whatever we are doing. Therefore, as many times as you can remember throughout the day, in whatever you find yourself doing, simply ask Jesus to do it in, with, and through you, to accomplish in you what He accomplished in the thirty years of His hidden life in Nazareth. Perhaps for now you can simply choose one specific activity you frequently do: whether changing diapers, hammering in nails, scanning items at a cash register, doing the dishes, or whatever else, and commit to do it from now on *in the Divine Will.* This can be done by saying or thinking, before said activity, *"Jesus wishes to do _____, therefore we will do _____ together,"* and then proceeding with deliberateness and a spirit of prayer, recollection, and consciousness of God's presence. The more acts you do in the Divine Will, the deeper into It you enter and the more you restore creation.

Does this still sound strange? Let us consider an analogy. When a man is building a chair and fastening the bolts together, he could honestly say, "my hands did that," but it would be better for him to say, *"I* did that." For when multiple powers concur in a single act, the greater rightly receives more recognition. While the soul of man is designed to enliven the flesh and command its acts, the Will of God can do much more: it can become the life of the acts of *another* free will that is distinct from Itself, and can do so without overriding or annihilating that other free will's operation. Although a great mystery, it becomes a reality through the Gift, so that just as the soul truly does what the body it gives life to does, the Divine Will does what the soul living in it does.

By doing our acts in the Divine Will, we can engage in another glorious invitation given to us through Luisa's revelations: *The Rounds*.

Do the Rounds

Before reciting the Sanctus—among the most highly exalted prayers—the Liturgy of the Church (in Eucharistic Prayer IV) instructs us to give **"voice to every creature under heaven."** It does not merely say that we give "thanks" for them, but rather demands that we ourselves truly give them a voice with our own prayers. And it is precisely this duty which Jesus' revelations to Luisa allow us to perform perfectly; for they do not merely invite us to pray for this or that intention nor do they merely reveal this or that new devotion; they go much further, inviting us to reacquire our rightful position as both the priests and the kings of creation, thus converting all created things into an explicit act of adoration. Before delving more deeply into Luisa's revelations on the matter, **we must now take a moment to, as we did with the Gift Itself, discover how the Rounds are themselves the perfectly fitting crown of a major and organic development that has long been growing in living Sacred Tradition.**

To begin this discovery, let us consider the Old Testament canticle of Daniel's companions who were thrown into the fire by Nebuchadnezzar, in which they repeatedly go through all manner of created things, calling upon each to "bless the Lord; praise and exalt him above all forever." (Daniel 3) This canticle is still in the public prayer of the Church in the Divine Office (the Liturgy of the Hours), the recitation of which is required of all clergy and religious. Although it is common to hear people lament the "repetitiveness" of the passage, such people miss the point entirely. God's purpose in inspiring these verses and in guiding the Church Universal to pray them constantly is not about intellectually recognizing the fact of Creation's mirroring of God's Glory; it is about, with one's will, going through all created things and *operating* this reality! In other words, this is real *work* to be *done* (albeit a work of pure joy), not mere *data* to be *memorized*. Similarly, would anyone who lives in a house on a mountaintop with breathtaking views always keep his blinds shut under the premise that he "already knows the view is beautiful and needn't bask in it all the time"? Certainly not. One could almost say such a resident has a duty to bless God constantly for the beauty he is so fortunate to be able to enjoy visually each day. But what worldly constraints prevent most of us from doing is nevertheless always accessible in spirit, through God's grace: by living in His Will and doing the Rounds. For in His Will, we do live on a mountaintop; but one more lofty and with a greater view—of past, present, and future; of all things in Creation,

Redemption, and Sanctification—thus, we have a far greater duty than a millionaire blessed with a mountaintop villa. But the Canticle in the Book of Daniel is not unique. The following authoritative citations speak to the same dynamic, and entire books could be filled with similar teachings:

"The soul leads all creation to the feet of its God and its Lord, that He may receive homage from every creature" – Blessed Marmion. **"Man is nature's priest"** – John Scotus Eriugena "Through his corporeality man unites in himself elements of the material world; these 'reach their summit through him, and through him raise their voice in free praise of the Creator'"– *Compendium of the Social Doctrine of the Church* §128 **"God willed that man be the king of creation."**–Pope St. John Paul II (October 29, 1983)

We see Pope Francis continuing in this same thread in the Magisterial teaching from his Encyclical *Laudato Si'*, of which a substantial excerpt is here needed with respect to how profound its overlap is with the Rounds as revealed to Luisa:

There is a mystical meaning to be found in a leaf, in a mountain trail, in a dewdrop, in a poor person's face … not because the finite things of this world are really divine, but because the mystic experiences the intimate connection between God and all beings … Standing awestruck before a mountain, he or she cannot separate this experience from God, and perceives that the interior awe being lived has to be entrusted to the Lord …Through our worship of God, we are invited to embrace the world on a different plane. …all the creatures of the material universe find their true meaning in the incarnate Word, for the Son of God has incorporated in his person part of the material world, planting in it a seed of definitive transformation … The world was created by the three Persons acting as a single divine principle, but each one of them performed this common work in accordance with his own personal property. Consequently, "when we contemplate with wonder the universe in all its grandeur and beauty, we must praise the whole Trinity." … **the Trinity has left its mark on all creation. Saint Bonaventure went so far as to say that human beings, before sin, were able to see how each creature** "testifies that God is three". The reflection of the Trinity was there to be recognized in nature "when that book was open to man and our eyes had not yet become darkened". … it could be readily contemplated if only the human gaze were not so partial, dark and fragile. … [The Pope closes the encyclical with the following prayer:] O Lord, seize us with your power and light, help us to protect all life, **to prepare for a better future, for the coming of your Kingdom** of justice, peace, love and beauty. Praise be to you! Amen. (§233-246)

The Pope himself is essentially here showing, in his very Magisterium, how to do the Rounds, and is telling us clearly that the Kingdom of God will come upon earth as a result of them! And he continued his teachings on this topic several years later, writing that, "In [the book that is creation], every creature becomes for us 'a word of God.'" (September 1, 2019) **St. Faustina was also keenly aware of the importance of this task of glorifying God on behalf of all creation, writing in her Diary, "I call on the whole universe to glorify Your mercy. Oh, how great is Your goodness, O God!"** (§1749) Within this entry, Faustina goes through all manner of created things and glorifies God on their behalf. This is the Rounds! And it is revealed clearly in the fully approved revelations to this canonized saint. Now that we can see how urgently these Rounds are needed and how orthodox they are, let us return to the exposition of them in Luisa's revelations. Fr. Iannuzzi teaches:

As man makes his "rounds" in creation by mystically penetrating, transforming and sublimating all creatures in God, there awakens in him a deep respect and awe for the world around him. He acquires a new set of eyes, as it were, with which he beholds all created things as a sacred extension of God's divine being and beauty. Because man in his desire to better the earth has taken from it without replenishing it, and has managed to disfigure it to the point of extinction, God reawakens within him the first impulse of love for the earth from which he came. Man was created for God through his relation to the earth, to its creatures and the cosmos. ... And so as the soul progresses in its love for God through the world around it, its vision of God extends not only to all created things, but to all events and all circumstances of life as well. (*The Splendor of Creation.* Ch 4)

In short: **Jesus wishes to find, in our own souls living in His Will, everything that He has done—in Creation, in Redemption, and in Sanctification.** How could it be otherwise? The whole point of Living in the Divine Will is that by way of this Gift, we are given by grace what God possesses by nature. But all is in God; therefore, all must be in us.

> My daughter, just **as all Creation is veil which hides my Will**, in the same way, my Humanity and all of my works, tears and pains are as many veils which hide my Supreme Fiat. It reigned in my acts, triumphant and dominating, and It laid the foundations in order to come to reign in the human acts of creatures. But do you know who tears these veils to let It come out to dominate in her own heart? One who recognizes It in each one of my acts, and invites It to come out. She **tears the veil of my works, she enters into them, she recognizes the noble Queen, and she prays It—she presses It to no longer remain hidden; and opening her heart to It, she invites It to enter.** (December 8, 1926)

In other words, the Gospel is not a mere history lesson. It is a presentation of living acts awaiting our own *Fiat* just like a marriage proposal awaits the same. Do not be frightened if heeding this offer seems like a task ill-suited to your talents, even if you consider them spiritually meager (I confess I have had the same reaction). Like the Gift Itself, the Rounds are operated simply by way of desiring and asking. Jesus tells Luisa:

> My very Divine Will, hidden in the created things, speaks by way of signs, as if It did not have speech. It speaks in the sun by way of signs of light and of heat; in the wind, giving penetrating and ruling signs; in the air It gives mute signs, such as to make Itself breath of all creatures. Oh! if the sun, the wind, the air and all other created things had the good of the word, how many things they would say to their Creator. **But, who is the speaking work of the Supreme Being? It is the [human] creature.** (February 13, 1931)

All creation is a revelation, but it lacks the ability to glorify its Creator *explicitly*. That task is left to us, the "speaking work" of the Supreme Being, for our very speaking of realities gives them new glories. This is certainly the case with the truths of the Faith: one of my favorite prayers has always been the Nicene Creed. Some might say, "that is not a prayer; it is merely a statement of Faith." I disagree! It is a prayer—a statement of Faith, yes, but so much more, if approached with the awe that is due to it. I have always felt like I am, in spirit, standing before the realities I affirm with my lips; gazing with wonder upon them and relishing the fact that I know of their validity with absolute certainty, impressing my own love and adoration upon them and offering them back to the God Who gave them. This approach to the Creed can inform our approach to the Rounds, in which we spiritually "re-do" all the acts of creation in the Will of God; approaching all that has transpired as a "Creed" of sorts.

With the Gift of Living in the Divine Will we can do this by visiting (in a spiritual bilocation of the soul, through our simple intention—not to be confused with any new-age idea related to "Astral Projection" or "remote viewing") all acts that have been done or will be done, and imprinting upon them our *Fiat*; our "I love You, I adore You, I glorify You, God." **In this, we subject all creation to the Divine Will and reorder it in** preparation for the Era, cooperating with God in setting *"creation free from its slavery to corruption."* (Romans 8:21) But not only do we give these gifts, as it were, to creation; we receive so much in return. Jesus tells Luisa:

> Now, when the soul has her interior book full, she will know very well the external book of the Divine Will. **All of Creation is nothing other than a book** of It; each created thing is a page that forms an immense book, and of many volumes. (July 6, 1931) My daughter, each created thing calls the creature to do the Divine Will ... In fact, each created thing carries out a distinct act of Divine Will, and with that act it calls the creature to do Its Divine Will. Each created thing has received from God, for this purpose, a special delight, in order to attract the creature in a mysterious way to do His Divine Will. (June 18, 1930)

Do you feel yourself lacking something—perhaps you know not even what? Immerse yourself—even if you can only afford to do so for a time—in the beauty of creation. A simple walk is often all it takes—perhaps in a park, a cemetery, or even just your backyard. **Learn from this beautiful Creation. Thank God for it. Bless God in its name. You will quickly find yourself attaining whatever it is you lacked.**

***

Now that we are hard at work receiving the Gift, acting in and through the Gift, and growing in the Gift—and thereby hastening the coming of the Kingdom as powerfully as possible—let us reassure ourselves that our efforts are guaranteed to bear their expected fruit. To that end, let us examine the multitude of reasons why this Era *must* come; reasons which readily present themselves to us if we look carefully at what God has been doing and saying for thousands of years.

†‡†

Chapter 3: Why Must the Era Come?

In considering what is to come on earth, we must above all remember one thing: *the greatest petition of the greatest prayer will not go unanswered.* Jesus, the Son of God, and indeed God Himself, knows all things and cannot lie. Not only did He promise that the Kingdom would come upon earth, but the only prayer He ever taught—the greatest prayer of Christianity—contains precisely this supplication as its very climax: **"Thy Kingdom come, Thy Will be done, on earth as It is in Heaven."** Jesus tells Luisa:

> If it were impossible that My Will could Reign on earth as in Heaven, My all Paternal Goodness would not have taught the Prayer of the Our Father, because to make impossible things prayed for, I would not have done...[and] I would have taught a prayer useless and without effect, and I do not know how to do useless things. At the most I wait even centuries, but I must make the fruit of My taught Prayer arise...Therefore, **everything I have manifested about My Will, is enclosed in these words alone: 'May Your Will be done on earth as It is in Heaven.'** (February 24, 1933) So after I formed [the Our Father] in the presence of My heavenly Father, certain that he would grant Me the Kingdom of My Divine Will on earth, I taught it to My apostles so that they might teach it to the whole world, and that one might be the cry of all: 'Your Will be done on earth as it is in heaven.' A promise more sure and solemn I could not make ... **it must come and souls must await it with the same certainty with which they awaited the future Redeemer. For My Divine Will is bound and committed to the words of the 'Our Father.' And when My Divine Will binds itself, whatever it promises is more than certain to come to pass.** Furthermore, since everything was prepared by Me, nothing else is needed but the manifestation of My Kingdom, which is what I am doing. (February 5, 1928)

Just as Creation came forth from God's hands in the beginning with nobility, beauty, and holiness, so too it will return to Him at the end of time in a similar state. Thus, the words of Revelation will be fulfilled, and the Church, the Bride of Christ, will ascend to the altar of God for the Great Wedding Feast that commences upon the consummation of history; not dirty, sick, and stained as she now is, but bejeweled and fully prepared "as a bride adorned for her husband," (Revelation 21:2) thanks to the Era of Peace. **"This is our great hope and our petition: 'Your Kingdom come'—a kingdom of peace, justice, and serenity, that will re-establish the original harmony of creation."** –Pope St. John Paul II

As John Paul teaches, the Original Harmony will be re-established on earth before the end. But the Original Harmony itself was ordered toward Heaven! We must therefore always remember that, far from eclipsing or duplicating Heaven, the Era holds, as its entire purpose, the aim of glorifying our Heavenly Fatherland. **While the Church will be rendered beautiful and glorious in the Era, her full perfection is only in Heaven; which we will await with *even more* eager longing during the Era than we do now.** For although during the Era the glory of the Church and the world will vastly outshine their present glory, we will also then be more cognizant of our ultimate destiny (the Beatific Vision of Heaven), thus our longing for it will increase in stride and far exceed its present degree, just as the closer a magnet is placed to a piece of steel, the stronger is the pull. Therefore, we will still be in an epic struggle towards our ultimate destiny in Heaven; but it will be a beautiful, victorious, glorious struggle instead of an ugly, despairing, miserable one we often observe in the world today (not, of course, that it has to be that way even now!).

To sum up all the preceding truths: *history requires symmetry.* **"Just as Creation started in an Outpouring of Love, in the same way, we will close it with Our children-in an Outpouring of Love."** (Jesus to Luisa. March 22, 1938) Jesus also tells Luisa:

> The end is my Will, because my Will was the beginning and, by justice, one who is the beginning must also be the end. Therefore, humanity must be enclosed in my Divine Volition to be given back her noble origin, her happiness, and to place the marriage with her Creator in force once again. Therefore, the great good that my Redemption did to man is not enough for Our love, but it yearns for more. True love never contents itself; only then is it content, when it can say: 'I have nothing else to give him.' (June 16, 1928)

Humanity must return to God in a similar state to that in which we came forth from Him. If we were to say this will not be so, then we blaspheme God by considering Him to be like ourselves; we who begin a task only to give up later with the end result being worse than that with which we started, like a worthless contractor who completes the demolition and brings in the new raw materials only to leave them all in a few piles around the house he was supposed to completely renovate. As the Canadian evangelist and author, Mark Mallett, put bluntly and accurately: **at the end of time, God's final words will not be *"Oh well, I tried."*** And Mark continues:

> Somehow, after thousands of years of salvation history, the suffering, death and Resurrection of the Son of God, the arduous journey of the Church and her saints through the centuries… I doubt those will be the Lord's words in the end… His promises will be fulfilled: creation will be renewed, although not perfectly until the end of human history. But within time, the Scriptures speak of a triumph of Christ in which His peace and Gospel will reach the ends of the earth… *Wisdom will be vindicated.* (markmallett.com/blog)

But at this point, perhaps the greatest obstacle is not so much a rational argument, but instead the simple vague temptation to doubt that so great a thing will ever come to be; for we are so used to disappointments. Luisa herself was not at all unlike those who today are tempted to doubt that the Divine Will could ever triumph on earth. One day, she thought to herself:

> "Nothing new, which is good, can be seen in the world. Sins have remained as they were; or, rather, they are worse… how can it ever be that, all of a sudden, man would give death to all vices, in order to give life to all virtues?" [Jesus responds to her, saying:] My daughter, yet, it will be so…Our Will will have Its return; It will have Its divine generations in the human will… At the most, it may take time; but the centuries will not end, until my Will obtains Its purpose. (June 18, 1925)

It *will* come. That is a guarantee. But now, let us from an eagle's-eye view of Church History observe how it, too, reveals with clarity that *now* is the perfect time for the arrival of the Era.

2,000 Years Have Carefully Prepared the Way for the Gift

In order to understand why our present age is at last the perfectly fitting time for the initiation of the Era, we must step back and examine the centuries-long growth of that which constitutes its essence. For although great and glorious will be the Era's qualities of peace, joy, beauty, happiness, and the like, its *essence* is found within its *sanctity* and all these qualities flow from that essence as effects from their cause. These mere effects do not require deep foundations labored over for centuries, for at the proper time they will easily flourish like fruits from a good tree—the tree itself, however, does require much work in preparing the soil. Therefore, we will only be misled if—upon looking to the left and to the right and seeing in the world only the continued degradation of peace, happiness, and all other goods that the Era will bring with it as effects—we conclude that the Era itself must be far off; just as we would only be likewise deluded if, upon observing the continued stiffening of the shell of a chrysalis during its development, we concluded that such rigidity overcoming the creature must entail the demise of any hope that it will become a being so endowed with beauty and vigor as a butterfly.

Escaping being so misled, therefore, will require that we dig deeper to discover what God Himself has *really* been busy at work doing throughout the history of the Church—inside, as it were, the chrysalis. **And this inner, essential work of God is *always* that which He undertakes *within* His few chosen souls, around whose littleness all the seemingly great and grand matters of the world revolve;** "grand" matters which, from the eternal perspective, are dwarfed by what is done in the souls of God's beloved. Does anyone who knows how the Incarnation transpired really need to be taught this lesson? Indeed, **for 2,000 years, the Holy Spirit has been—within these chosen souls—building the foundations of the Era's sanctity, and precisely the time in which we now live is the fitting one for the bestowal the crown of His efforts; that is, the Crown of Sanctity.** (This dynamic has been traced out in much more detail on pages 115 to 173 in *The Crown of Sanctity*.)

Now, even in the days of the Old Testament, God was preparing the foundations for His greatest desire: to give His very own Life to His children—that is, the Gift of His Will. Or rather, He was doing so from the very beginning and always had this as His aim; for, as Aquinas teaches, "although the end be last in the order of execution, yet it is first in the order of intention." (*Summa Theologica* I-II. QI. AI) But in mankind's earliest days, the reverberations of the sanctity of Eden were sufficient to long maintain him in peace and justice. Once these emanations diminished, however, evil began to dominate, and starting again by means of a universal flood became necessary. Upon this now clean slate, God began preparing to give—4,000 years later—His Will again, even more gloriously than He had done in the very beginning. He began this laborious process by putting in place the first step to Living in His Will; namely, revealing some key elements of its contents and demanding obedience thereto. Thus it was that the just life, though accessible to reason, was revealed to Moses and great promises accompanied its faithful observance. But God ultimately desired loving sons, not merely obedient servants. So, when the fullness of time had come, He sent His own only begotten Son to earth in order that all who loved Him could be incorporated into His very Body and receive adopted sonship. Consequently, this work of preparing for the Gift exploded in intensity upon the Incarnation of the Word of God and the founding of Christianity, as we see in the following Scriptural verses.

"You may escape from the corruption that is in the world because of passion, and become partakers of the divine nature."(2 Peter 1:4) The literature which exists merely for the sake of meditating on the implications of the words, "partakers of the divine nature," could fill volumes—its authors understanding that there is no escaping that here, St. Peter—and thus the Holy Spirit Who is inspiring these words of Scripture—is teaching something radical about the degree to which God wills to transform us.

"It is no longer I who live, but Christ who lives in me." (Galatians 2:20) This, too, is utterly radical. It is not achieved simply by a "personal relationship" with Jesus Christ, as if the union Christ calls us to is as "safe" as the union one may have with a friend on social media; it is achieved only by a total, holding-*nothing*-back death to self.

"Let the same mind be in you that was in Christ Jesus." (Philippians 2:5) As a professor, I would rightly be called insane if I told my students that, in order to pass the test I am about to give them, they must have *my same mind* in them. St. Paul is of course not merely teaching that we must be good students of Christ; rather, he is teaching that our own minds truly can be absorbed into Jesus' mind—and, thus, the Divine Mind—so truly that it cannot even be said we operate with separate minds.

"See what love the Father has given us, that we should be called children of God; and so we are." (I John 3:1) **"God sent forth his Son, born of woman ... so that we might receive adoption as sons... through God you are no longer a slave but a son."** (Galatians 4:4-7) Some throughout the history of the Church have written this teaching off as only a use of metaphorical language. But they are wrong. It is not *metaphorical*, but is, rather, *literally true*, that we may be made into children of God. Obviously, none of us is or ever can be the Uncreated Second Person of the Blessed Trinity, as Jesus Christ alone is. Nevertheless, our sonship is an assertion of our possession—by grace, not by nature—of all that which is essential to sonship. And just as any good father who adopted a child would rightly rebuke another for claiming that the sonship of this child was a metaphor, so too we mustn't detract from the glory and truth of our own divine sonship with such a reductionistic approach unworthy of the reality at hand.

Already, from this small handful of Scriptural verses, we can see that God was embarking upon a bold quest by increasing the heights of sanctity now available; a quest He did not abandon upon the death of the last Apostle and the concomitant completion of Public Revelation, but rather continued as zealously as ever in *The Four Great Paradigms* of Sacred Tradition.

For even the unfathomable Divine Intervention that is the Incarnation and Redemption did not change the fact that God always operates in an organic way; that is, *step by step*. To reveal the Gift in all its fullness at their time would have been artificial; like trying to teach Calculus to a student just beginning Algebra. Indeed, the whole essence of Calculus is contained, seminally, within Algebra itself and no new (analogous) "public revelation" is needed to progress from one to the other. But much time and effort *are* needed to gradually render more explicit what was only subtle from the start. This is not at all to say that the first Christians themselves were less holy than today's Christians—in fact, the opposite seems quite obviously true. The point is merely that much growth of the Church *as a whole Mystical Body* was needed; just as for example, much more growth was also needed before the Church was likewise ready for the Rosary, the Marian Dogmas, or the spirituality of St. Thérèse of Lisieux. In sum, **although 2,000 years ago was truly the *fullness of time*, it nevertheless was not the ripe time to reveal the Gift in all Its clarity and invite the nascent Church into It**—but only to reveal Its beginnings. And even though they are beginnings, we have seen that what they *point to* is in no way unclear. Realizing this, the greatest minds and the greatest saints in the history of the Church have built upon these beginnings to help make ever clearer—within the forthcoming Four Great Paradigms—the Gift's implicit references in Scripture. Providence has orchestrated this movement so that once these Paradigms have been sufficiently promulgated and understood, their crown—the Gift—may be bestowed upon the Church through Luisa's revelations. We turn now to the Paradigms themselves.

The Four Great Paradigms: Invitations to the Gift

Building over the centuries like the crescendo of a classical masterpiece, we see the foundations of sanctity as laid down in Scripture being more and more deeply understood until the present day, in which we are at last ready for the fruit of all these labors (the Gift). Let us, then, acquaint ourselves with the nature of the build-up of this crescendo, which is seen in four paradigms that constitute God's Four Great Invitations which He offers in preparing the way for the Universal Reign of the Divine Will. **These are not merely separate apostolates or movements, but are rather four prongs of the same Divine Attack to cast out the prince of this world (the devil), win back the world for God, and restore all things in Christ.** These four prongs, invitations, or paradigms are: **Divinization,** as found in virtually all the Fathers of the Church; **Mystical Marriage,** as found in many Doctors of the Church; the spirituality of the **Unification of Wills,** as found in the French spirituality of the 17th through 19th centuries that found their pinnacle in the teachings of St. Thérèse of Lisieux; and **Marian Consecration,** as popularized especially by St. Louis de Montfort.

Providentially, in each of these four paradigms, we find in their nature a "pointing;" that is, an indication that they themselves are directed to some result beyond themselves. For "Divinization" (also known as "Deification") implies a *process* ("-tion") which calls for some culmination. Mystical marriage, or spiritual marriage, as a marriage indeed, is ordered towards the generation of children, thus it calls for a fruitfulness beyond itself. The Unification of Wills always calls for, just as any unification does, not just correspondence but also a total merging and fusion of the two unified things, as the water dropped into the chalice at the Mass becomes inseparable from the wine therein. And Marian Consecration, if it is to reach its fulfillment, requires a likeness—a true similarity in the most important way and a veritable sharing of life—between the one being consecrated and the one to whom consecration is directed. **So, these four great paradigms—while each deserves enormous exaltation on its own right—are nevertheless essentially invitations.** *They are invitations to the Gift of Living in the Divine Will.*

Divinization: The Foundation

Early in Church History, the concept of the **Divinization, Deification, or Theosis of Man**, long spoken of especially in Eastern Catholic Mysticism, speaks in a way that beautifully foreshadows Luisa's revelations. Though neglected for a time, this teaching is finally making a comeback. The Catechism teaches, "Constituted in a state of holiness, **man was destined to be fully 'divinized' by God in glory.**" (§398) Dr. Scott Hahn, in his foreword to *Called to be the Children of God*, writes:

> Jesus saves us from sin and death. Rescue from sin and death is indeed a wonderful thing— but the salvation won for us by Jesus Christ is incomparably greater… Even in the Catholic Church, the idea of divinization got lost amid all the post-Reformation disputes over the relationship of faith, works, and justification. For four centuries, Catholic and Protestant theologians alike focused so narrowly on these controversies that they obscured the central fact of Christian salvation…

This is in no way to detract from the immense importance, which cannot possibly be overstated, of the Redemption and of the application of the graces of Redemption to individuals for their salvation. This remains the foundation, and the Church Fathers knew that: but they also knew this was the beginning, not the end, of the spiritual life. To better understand their outlook, let us consider some specific teachings of the Fathers on this matter. Before presenting several quotes from other Fathers of the Church, however, a few general words on St. Athanasius are in order. *The Great Exchange*, "God was made man that we might be made God," quoted in the Catechism (§460), comes to us first, and most explicitly, from him—that great Father and Doctor of the Church who is fondly remembered as the heroic defender of the Divinity of Christ against the onslaught of the Arian heresy. Sadly, however, his mysticism is often forgotten. The Catechism's revival of this quote from Athanasius, therefore, was no doubt Providential. As many continue to turn to his intercession and example in order to confront the crisis in the Church today, let us ensure that we do not lose sight of **the entire purpose of the Christological orthodoxy which Athanasius fought for; namely, that we too become "other Christs."**

> **Augustine.** [Contained within the Divine Office is his famous teaching on Divinization:] Beloved, our Lord Jesus Christ, the eternal creator of all things, today became our Savior by being born of a mother. Of his own will he was born for us today, in time, so that he could lead us to his Father's eternity. **God became man so that man might become God.** The Lord of the angels became man today so that man could eat the bread of angels. (Office of Readings. Saturday before Epiphany)
>
> **Gregory of Nazianzus:** Let us become God's for His sake, since He for ours became Man. (*Oration* I Paragraph V) For He still pleads even now as Man for my salvation; for He continues to wear the Body which He assumed, until He make me God by the power of His Incarnation. (*Oration* 30 Paragraph XIV) While His inferior Nature, the Humanity, became

God, because it was united to God, and became One Person because the Higher Nature prevailed in order that I too might be made God so far as He is made Man. (*Oration* 29. Chapter XIX)

Irenaeus: [T]he Word of God, our Lord Jesus Christ, who did, through His transcendent love, become what we are, that He might bring us to be even what He is Himself... For it was necessary, at first, that nature should be exhibited; then, after that, that what was mortal should be conquered and swallowed up by immortality, and the corruptible by incorruptibility, and that man should be made after the image and likeness of God. (*Against Heresies*. Book V)

Clement of Alexandria: The Word of God became man, that thou mayest learn from man how man may become God. ... For the Word Himself is the manifest mystery: God in man, and man God...He who listens to the Lord, and follows the prophecy given by Him, will be formed perfectly in the likeness of the teacher—made a god going about in flesh. (*Exhortation to the Heathen*. Chapter I)

Hippolytus of Rome: And you shall be a companion of the Deity, and a co-heir with Christ, no longer enslaved by lusts or passions... For you have become God: for whatever sufferings you underwent while being a man, these He gave to you, because you were of mortal mould, but whatever it is consistent with God to impart, these God has promised to bestow upon you, because you have been deified, and begotten unto immortality. (*Refutation of All Heresies*. Book X. Chapter 30)

Gregory of Nyssa: By this communion with Deity mankind might at the same time be deified, for this end it is that, by dispensation of His grace, He disseminates Himself in every believer through that flesh, whose substance comes from bread and wine, blending Himself with the bodies of believers, to secure that, by this union with the immortal, man, too, may be a sharer in incorruption. For just as He in Himself assimilated His own human nature to the power of the Godhead, being a part of the common nature, but not being subject to the inclination to sin which is in that nature... so, also, will He lead each person to union with the Godhead. (*The Great Catechism*. Part III. Chapter 37)

Clear as it now is that the Divinization of Man is essential to Christianity as rightly understood by the Fathers, we can still see that it is essentially an invitation to something else that lies outside of its own domain as described by these Fathers. As Cardinal Schonborn teaches, "**Deification is located in the reestablishing of fallen man in his innate dignity,**"[19] a re-establishment that would not be fully discovered until Luisa's revelations. These Fathers rightly grasped that Christianity, in its inescapable essence, is ordered toward the Divinization of the Christian. But this process, this Diviniza-*tion*, required much more development over the course of the centuries of Sacred Tradition before its nature could be rendered more explicit and its object thereby more readily attained. This development was provided by the great mystical Doctors following the Patristic Era, to whom we presently turn.

Mystical Marriage: The Development

In St. Bernard of Clairvaux, Doctor of the Church and "last of the Fathers," (though strictly speaking not counted among their ranks), we see a bridge to the next era in the development of the Church's spiritual theology. Pope Pius XII, who gave him the aforementioned title, taught that perhaps no one has spoken more excellently on Divine Charity than he (cf. *Doctor Mellifluus* §17). For Bernard, too, spoke of the Deification of man, but rightly taught that it consists in a transformation based on the love of God (cf. *On Loving God*), and his teachings enabled the saints who followed him to describe this Divinization, more precisely, as a veritable *mystical marriage*. In his masterpiece,

Spiritual Theology, Fr. Jordan Aumann describes mystical marriage as follows:

> The soul becomes brilliant and transformed in God, and God communicates to the soul his supernatural being to such an extent that the soul appears to be God and to have all that God has. ... The soul seems to be more God than soul and is truly God by participation. (§ 12)

Being that it is clearly such a tremendous sanctity, it is unsurprising that mystical marriage, up to the 20th century, had generally been seen as the definitive triumph of the spiritual life of a soul on earth, constituting the highest degree of sanctity possible for a wayfarer, but given only to extremely few saints throughout Church History. This supremacy is not difficult to discover; to give one example, the old Catholic Encyclopedia makes it clear, saying, "The term mystical marriage is employed by St. Teresa and St. John of the Cross to designate that mystical union with God which is *the most exalted condition attainable by the soul in this life.*" But, we should bear in mind—and this is acknowledged in the writings of St. John of the Cross and St. Teresa of Avila, the two greatest writers on mystical marriage—that while it was considered the highest state of sanctity possible *on earth,* **it was not even then considered the highest state of sanctity *possible*.** It is never denied, in all the most trustworthy writings on mystical and spiritual theology, that the state of sanctity of the blessed in Heaven is nevertheless superior. (And Jesus makes it equally clear to Luisa and to other mystics of the 20th century—as we will see in the next section—that it is precisely this Heavenly sanctity which He is now freely giving to those who yearn for it.)

For we can see upon a simple examination that this reality of mystical marriage clearly points to something. All acknowledge that natural marriage is intrinsically ordered toward something beyond itself: the procreation of children. Mystical marriage, too—inasmuch as the mystical life is an authentic reflection of earthly realities, which in fact it is—must be ordered towards something beyond itself. For although it is possible to take any analogy too far, it would be strange for one so essential as spiritual marriage (a simile chosen by God Himself in describing what He has wrought in the lives of the saints) to fail to remain analogous on such an important property. Indeed, even before Jesus revealed the Gift clearly to the mystics of the 20th century, there was a sense that perhaps there is something higher still, theoretically attainable on earth, exceeding this "third stage" (the unitive way) of the spiritual life, which finds its own height in mystical marriage. Hugh Owen writes, drawing from several theologians:

> The traditional division of the spiritual life into three stages—the purgative, illuminative, and unitive—had obscured the existence of a fourth stage where the transforming union of the soul and God produced its supernatural fruit. "It would be absurd actually, if, when the soul reaches the highest union on earth, its life would stagnate, that it would remain permanently inactive. Just the contrary happens; that is the time when the action of the soul, under the motion of the Holy Spirit, reaches its maximum. This is the fourth stage ... In the transforming union, the soul is united with the Word. But this union is spiritually fecund; its fruit is Jesus, Jesus reproduced in the soul itself."[20]

A profound picture emerges: Mystical Marriage—the pinnacle of the highest stage of the spiritual life—though truly Deifying in its own right and hitherto considered the highest degree of sanctity possible on earth, nevertheless on closer consideration seems ordered to something else. Giving a hint as to where this superior "something" resides, St. John of the Cross writes:

The entire matter of reaching union with God consists in purging the will of its appetites and emotions so that **from a human and lowly will it may be changed into the divine will**, made identical with the will of God. (*Ascent of Mt Carmel. Book III*, Ch. 16, §3)

Let us now consider this central insight of St. John; for it is the very insight that allowed for the flourishing of the spirituality of the following centuries in the Third Paradigm, the Paradigm which, in turn, perfectly disposes those who heed it for the Gift.

Unification of Wills: The Insight

During the 17th century, a growing understanding in spiritual theology recognized that—despite the commendable explosion of intellect-centered scholasticism in the preceding centuries—the true essence, beginning, and end of the spiritual life revolved around the will: specifically, the total unreserved handing over of the human will to the Divine Will. For it is in so handing over the will, that love is most demonstrated, and in which love finds its completion. The more this fact was understood, the more forcefully the great spiritual writers promulgated the teaching, and the more carefully they centralized their writings around it:

St. Francis de Sales, *Doctor of the Church*: So the soul that loves God is so transformed into the divine will, that it merits rather to be called, God's will, than to be called, obedient and subject to his will. ...**among the true children of our Saviour, every one shall forsake his own will, and shall have only one master-will, dominant and universal, which shall animate, govern and direct all souls, all hearts and all wills... [transforming] them all into itself**; so that the will of Christians and the will of Our Lord may be but one single will. ... Ah! who will give my soul the grace of having no will save the will of her God! (*Treatise on the Love of God.* Ch. VIII)

St. Alphonsus Liguori, *Doctor of the Church*: Perfection is founded entirely on the love of God... and perfect love of God means the complete union of our will with God's ...Mortification, meditation, receiving Holy Communion, acts of fraternal charity are all certainly pleasing to God—but only when they are in accordance with his will. When they do not accord with God's will, he not only finds no pleasure in them, but he even rejects them utterly and punishes them. ...During our sojourn in this world, we should learn from the saints now in heaven, how to love God. The pure and perfect love of God they enjoy there, consists in uniting themselves perfectly to his will. ... Our Lord himself teaches us to ask to do the will of God on earth as the saints do it in heaven: "Thy will be done on earth as it is in heaven." ...A single act of uniformity with the divine will suffices to make a saint...We cannot offer God anything more pleasing than to say: Take us, Lord, we give thee our entire will. ... [but] **let us not only strive to conform ourselves... Conformity signifies that we join our wills to the will of God. Uniformity means more—it means that we make one will of God's will and ours, so that we will only what God wills; that God's will alone, is our will**. This is the summit of perfection and to it we should always aspire... [and invoke] our mother Mary, the most perfect of all the saints because she most perfectly embraced the divine will. (*Uniformity with God's Will* Ch. I)

Fr. Caussade: If [souls that tend towards sanctity only] understood that to attain the utmost height of perfection, the safest and surest way is submission to the will of God which changes into divine gold all their occupations, troubles, and sufferings, what consolation would be theirs! ... O my God! how much I long to be the missionary of Your holy will, and to teach all men that there is nothing more easy, more attainable, more within reach, and in the power of everyone, than sanctity. ...Oh! All you that read this, it will cost you no more than to do what you are doing, to suffer what you are suffering, only act and suffer in a holy manner. It is the heart that must be changed. When I say heart, I mean will. **Sanctity, then, consists in willing all that God wills for us. Yes! Sanctity of heart is a simple "fiat," a conformity of will with the will of God**. (*Abandonment to Divine Providence* § IX)

As is so clear from the quotes above, in this spirituality of Union of Wills we see the *perfect* preparation for the Gift of *Living in* the Divine Will. If anyone feels, for whatever reason, unprepared to open Luisa's revelations, then he should pick up any one of the three books quoted above (each of unassailable orthodoxy and universally regarded as essential to Catholic spirituality), read them from cover to cover, and he will then find his thirst for more knowledge of the Divine Will enkindled. I can testify that in my own case, God led me to St. Alphonsus' work quoted above and—long before I had heard anything of Luisa—convicted me that it contained the ultimate key to the spiritual life. For, indeed, it did. The *conformity* of wills preached by the Scholastics (especially Aquinas) is the key to the *Uniformity* of Wills preached by the great Doctors of the 17th to 19th centuries, which in turn is the key to the *Living* in the Divine Will revealed to the 20th-century mystics (above all, Luisa).

It is no accident that **the summit of this spirituality, which we find in the Little Way of St. Thérèse of Lisieux, was first published (in *The Story of a Soul,* September 30, 1898) a mere six months before the Church gave Luisa the order to write down her revelations from Jesus** (on February 28, 1899). In an obedience identical to that of Thérèse's own (who was likewise ordered to write her diary), Luisa commenced. God wastes no time and with Him there are no coincidences.

These great spiritual masters, however, could not describe how this perfect and complete union they so desired goes about happening. How can the human will really be fused with the Divine Will? What effects does this fusion—this *living in*—entail? What else does it teach us? What do we "do" with it? They knew that this union is necessary, but they could not tell us how exactly to achieve it except by rightly exhorting us to accept the Will of God in all things and desire nothing but what He desires. This is no mark against them: their works were orchestrated by Providence for their own sake, indeed, but also as preparations for Luisa's revelations, which *do* tell us about that in which this fusion of wills consists. But there is still one more Paradigm to consider. This last Paradigm is more than just a preparation—it is perhaps more accurately called a *catalyst* for the Gift's explosion throughout the whole world. In his own introduction to Caussade's masterpiece quoted above, Dom Arnold, OSB, leads us to this final Paradigm, Marian Consecration:

The "Abandonment to Divine Providence" … is a trusting, childlike, peaceful abandonment to the guidance of grace, and of the Holy Spirit: an unquestioning and undoubting submission to the holy will of God in all things that may befall us, be they due to the action of man, or to the direct permission of God. **To Fr. de Caussade, abandonment to God, the "Ita Pater" of our Divine Lord, the "Fiat" of our Blessed Lady, is the shortest, surest, and easiest way to holiness and peace.**

Marian Consecration: The Catalyst

Of the Four Great Invitations or Paradigms, Marian Consecration is the final and definitive blow to the human will; thus, making straight the way for the Reign of the Divine Will both in individuals and, soon, over the whole world. The other three of the Great Invitations have been popular in the spiritual theology of the Church for some time, but **Marian Consecration has exploded in popularity only recently. This explosion has** been caused by God in order to serve as the immediate precursor to the Gift of Living in the Divine Will, which too shall soon explode throughout the world. One who consecrates himself to Our Lady, and consequently becomes clothed in her very own virtues—as the Father of Marian Consecration, St. Louis de Montfort, promised such a soul would be so clothed—cannot but live in the Divine Will. For it is precisely this type of life that is the essence of her sanctity and is therefore also the Gift she earnestly desires to mediate to all her children. This great saint was also aware of the fact that when this spirituality spread, it would form the greatest saints of the end of the Era and usher in the Reign of Peace; so much so that he even formally prophesied it, writing:

> Almighty God and his holy Mother are to raise up great saints who will surpass in holiness most other saints as much as the cedars of Lebanon tower above little shrubs …They will be exceptionally devoted to the Blessed Virgin. Illumined by her light, strengthened by her food, guided by her spirit …Mary has produced, together with the Holy Ghost, the greatest thing which has been or ever will be—a God-man; and **she will consequently produce the greatest saints that there will be** …They shall be great and exalted before God in sanctity… with the humility of their heel, in union with Mary, they shall crush the head of the devil and **cause Jesus Christ to triumph.** (*True Devotion to Mary* §46-48)

St. Louis de Montfort died in 1716, but his legacy lives on and his impact has only continued to grow. In the past several years especially, Marian Consecration has deservedly begun to dominate the scene of Catholic spirituality. Earlier in the last century we saw St. Maximilian Kolbe's efforts in his Militia Immaculata blessed abundantly by providence, but more recently, millions of Catholics around the world have consecrated themselves to Mary; many in response to the "My Consecration" apostolate of the late hero of Our Lady's causes, Anthony Mullen, as well as Fr. Michael Gaitley's *33 Days to Morning Glory*. And what does this consecration now dominating the Church entail? The Franciscan Friars of the Immaculate give an overview; in which we find the following:

> By this consecration, one offers himself wholly to Our Lady… a complete surrender of self into Our Lady's hands. From the moment of consecration, she is to enter the life of the person in order to completely Marianize it—to transform it according to her ways. The consecrated person ought to succeed in "living with Mary, for Mary, in Mary" … [another] form of consecration is inspired by the Little Flower's offering of herself as a victim of Jesus' merciful love, and it expresses principally the total immolation, the complete sacrifice, of oneself to God, to become like Mary when she totally sacrificed herself in the exercise of generous, merciful love. Identical in substance, each of these forms of consecration is intended to make us carry out a filial devotion to Our Lady in the most deep-rooted, radical way. They mean to make us sink our roots into Mary's Heart with the happy certainty that "he who plants his roots in Mary becomes holy" (St. Bonaventure). The experience the saints have had assures us that this is quite true. (Marymediatrix.com)

Clearly, so many souls undertaking this heroic consecration will not go unnoticed by Heaven, nor will such a great movement as this go unrewarded in the world. But even Marian Consecration—glorious as it is—was not fully capable of alone bestowing its ultimate aim upon those who undertook it before the 20th century; nor did the writers who expounded upon it before that time fully grasp its enormity, since its enormity and primary end is indeed the Gift Itself. We can see this by examining the development presented by the teachings of St. Maximilian Kolbe who, since he did live in the 20th century, was capable of (and clearly succeeded in) receiving and relaying the Gift. St.

Maximilian Kolbe is most often recalled as the heroic martyr of charity, killed at the infamous concentration camp at Auschwitz, as he willingly volunteered himself to take the place of another man. Struck by Our Lady's words at Lourdes, "I am *the* Immaculate Conception," Kolbe came to the recognition that this was no grammatical mistake. He realized that these words said something essential about Mary herself: that she *is the* Immaculate Conception, and truly a mirror of the *Uncreated* Immaculate Conception, Who is none other than the Holy Spirit. He furthermore realized that Mary is simply the *Created* Immaculate Conception—the perfect creature contained within the mind of God before the dawn of time, destined before all ages to be the Mother of the Word (for, as we will see in the following chapter, the Incarnation was an eternal decree of God; not a "Plan B" that was enacted merely due to the Fall). But Kolbe did not stop there; he insisted that through Mary, this reality must define our sanctity as well. St. Maximilian wrote:

> We are hers without limits, most perfectly hers; we are, as it were, herself... may she herself think, speak, and act through us. We want to belong to such an extent to the Immaculate that not only nothing else remains in us that isn't hers, but that we become, as it were, annihilated in her, changed into her, transubstantiated into her, that she alone remains, so that we may be as much hers as she is God's. ... What a magnificent mission! ... Divinizing man to the God-Man through the Mother of the God-Man.[21]

Here, St. Maximilian reaps the fruit of the tree which St. Louis de Montfort planted: that **the ultimate purpose of Marian consecration is not only to be totally devoted *to* her, but rather, to "*become* her;" with the only differences being somewhat superficial, or in other words (and to continue with the "transubstantiation" teaching), the differences are mere accidents.** While we of course cannot use the term "transubstantiation" here in exactly the same way we use it in reference to the Blessed Sacrament—wherein the former substance of the thing in question is completely *replaced* by an entirely new and different substance—we nevertheless cannot write this teaching off as mere exaggeration or hyperbole, either. Fr. Fehlner writes, explaining this teaching of Kolbe:

> This relation he explains in precise, dogmatic detail, as an intimate union or communion of two persons and two natures, the persons and natures remaining really distinct, yet so intimate that the whole being and person of the Immaculate is permeated through and through by that characteristic of the Spirit ... of Father and Son as to be herself "transubstantiated" into the Holy Spirit and to share his name. ... far from being the dangerous formula some see in it, is an original, yet deeply traditional insights of St. Maximilian... Being [Mary's] property [Kolbe] defines as our being annihilated in Her, changed into Her, transubstantiated into Her, so as it were to be Her... **Another word to describe this promotion of the cause of the Immaculate is marianization, or the Fiat, which with that of the Creator effects the recreation or new creation.** [22]

Addressing this clear development that we find in St. Maximilian, Hugh Owen writes:

> St. Maximilian's insights into the sanctity of Our Lady represented a definite development beyond the insights recorded in the writings of St. Louis De Montfort. ... St. Louis conceived of the union between Our Lady and the Holy Spirit as a moral union. But St. Maximilian realized that this concept did not do justice to their relationship. According to theologian Manteau-Bonamy: "Father Kolbe ... knew that de Montfort, who never heard of the apparitions of the Rue du Bac or of Lourdes, had remained limited to the consideration of a moral bond between Mary and the Holy Spirit. But since it is perfectly possible to understand the union which St. de Montfort writes about, in the meaning it acquired at Lourdes, Father

Kolbe does not hesitate to interpret it so." (*New and Divine.* 101)

It is safe to say that, from its beginning, Marian Consecration was always ordered to this type of Marian life that is just another name for the Gift of Living in the Divine Will (for to have Mary's life is to have Jesus' life). But with the advent of the clear revelation of the Gift in Luisa's writings, its full potential can now at last be attained. This most avowedly does not mean that Marian Consecration should be "moved on from"—on the contrary, it means quite the opposite: we should now approach Marian Consecration with even more love and more zeal, knowing that it can truly deliver *fully* on all of its promises!

***

Understanding these Four Great Invitations is necessary for one's personal benefit in receiving the Gift: one is more than ready to receive the Gift of Living in the Divine Will by taking all Four Invitations seriously and obeying their instructions. It is also necessary in order to see how perfectly the Gift fits in to the Sacred Tradition of the Church, for it shows how this moment is the opportune time for God to make haste in giving It. Let us now turn to see where the Gift is revealed outside of the pages of Luisa's own revelations.

The Gift Permeating 20th-Century Mysticism

Even if we set aside Luisa's revelations for a moment, it is impossible to miss what Heaven is calling us to today through the consensus of the mysticism of those to whom it speaks most clearly. For if, as Jesus tells Luisa, giving the Gift is God's greatest desire (and indeed it is), then it would only be natural to expect to see intimations of this desire within the writings of those mystics who also lived during the Age of the Gift (that is, from 1889—when Luisa first received It—onwards). Such intimations do not detract from Luisa's status as the primary herald and earthly head of this Gift. (Similarly, St. Faustina is certainly the primary herald of the Divine Mercy; and yet, we see the same essential insights into the Divine Mercy permeating private revelations particularly from the time of the Sacred Heart revelations to St. Margaret Mary Alacoque onward.) Instead, they simply verify the importance of this great Divine Intervention by confirming what one would expect to see if it is authentic.

And, indeed, those who desire this verification of authenticity will be pleased to hear that **the main thrust of Luisa's revelations, and even many of their specifics, have already been asserted by many other mystics of the 20th century (equally tellingly, in accordance with the real newness of this Gift, *nowhere* in Church History can they be found before 1889).** Many of these mystics have already received so much approval and ecclesiastical approbation that no one has any grounds to doubt them, and we now turn to consider a small sample of their teachings. (Although only four such mystics are covered here, a multitude in fact exist; for example, Servant of God Archbishop Luis Martinez, Vera Grita, Servant of God Sr. Mary of the Holy Trinity, Fr. George Kosicki, Servant of God Fr. Walter Ciszek, and many others. St. Maximilian Kolbe was particularly acutely aware of the Gift as It relates to and is naturally demanded by Marian Consecration, but since we covered these teachings of his in the previous section, we will not do so again here.)

St. Faustina: Transconsecration of the Self Into a Living Host

Considering the extraordinary levels of not only Ecclesiastical approbation, but veritable Ecclesiastical exaltation, that St. Faustina's revelations have received, we can be completely confident that whatever is revealed within her Diary is in fact true; still a private revelation, of course, but a thoroughly trustworthy one. In this Diary, we read:

> The soul receiving this **unprecedented grace of union with God** cannot say that it sees God face to face, because even here there is a very thin veil of faith, but so very thin that the soul can say that it sees God and talks with Him. It is "divinized." God allows the soul to know how much He loves it, and the soul sees that **better and holier souls than itself have not received this grace.** Therefore, it is filled with holy amazement, which maintains it in deep humility, and it steeps itself in its own nothingness and holy astonishment. (§771)

St. Faustina describes Living in the Divine Will here quite accurately with the term "unprecedented grace"—for that is exactly what It is (a *new* and divinizing sanctity to renew the world, as Pope St. John Paul II described It). Despite knowing nothing of Luisa, and not herself being the one instructed by God on the Gift, Faustina here in fact answers the first concern that some people have about the Gift of Living in the Divine Will, namely, *"How could I, who am so unworthy, receive a Gift so much greater than what was received by the saints of days past who dwarf me in virtue?"* Well, *because it is a gift!* It doesn't make *you* better; it simply gives you a greater gift without changing the fact that you are less deserving of it than those better souls who nevertheless did not receive it. Later in St. Faustina's revelations, we read the words of Jesus:

> My beloved child, delight of My Heart, your words are dearer and more pleasing to me than the angelic chorus… [your] smallest act of virtue has unlimited value in My eyes because of your great love for Me. In a soul that lives on My love alone, I reign as in heaven. … rest a moment near My Heart and taste of the love in which you will delight for all eternity. (§1489) [Faustina relates:] **"The veils of mystery hinder me not at all; I love You as do Your chosen ones in heaven."** (§1324) **"I live Your divine life as do the elect in heaven…"** (§1393)

Here, we see Jesus revealing to Faustina that she was given precisely what the Gift Itself is fundamentally defined as: **the life of Heaven, now capable of being lived on earth**; what St. John of the Cross called "the perfect state of glory," which he thought was reserved for Heaven, but which we now see can be received by us pilgrims on earth. Jesus furthermore tells Faustina that her acts are more meritorious—more pleasing to Him— than all the angels are in themselves. This is what the Gift of Living in the Divine Will does—It makes our acts truly unlimited in their value, as Faustina here says, which means that even the angels cannot hope to please God as we can with the Gift. Later, St. Faustina wrote: "When I unite myself with Your will, O Lord, **Your power works through me and** *takes the place* of my feeble will." (§650) **It is this Divine Substitution we receive in the Gift of Living in the Divine Will.** But earlier still in the Diary, St. Faustina describes a profound turning point in her life. While at the convent, she was asked by Jesus to give her consent to become a victim soul. A profound exchange follows:

> I said, "Do with me as You please. I subject myself to Your will. As of today, Your holy will shall be my nourishment" … I was [then] extraordinarily **fused with God** …A great mystery took place during that adoration, a mystery between the Lord and myself. … And the Lord said to me, 'You are the delight of My Heart; from today on, every one of your acts, even the very smallest, will be a delight to My eyes, whatever you do.' At that moment I felt **transconsecrated. My earthly body was the same, but my soul was different; God was now living in it with the totality of His delight.** This is not a feeling, but a conscious reality that nothing can obscure. (§136-137)

"Transconsecration" is not a word you will often hear, but it is a wonderful name for the Gift of Living in the Divine Will. By using this word (and it appears she may have been the first), St. Faustina dares to say that what occurs within the host during the Mass has occurred within her soul as well. Jesus tells Luisa the same. Elsewhere in Faustina's revelations, we read the following:

[Jesus says:] "**Host** pleasing to My Father, know, My daughter, that the entire Holy Trinity finds Its special delight in you, because **you live exclusively by the will of God**. No sacrifice can compare with this." ... [Faustina responds:] The pure offering of my will will burn on the altar of love... Let all my desires, even the holiest, noblest and most beautiful, take always the last place and Your holy will, the very first. (§955-957) [Faustina prayed:] I beg You, by all the love with which Your Heart burns, to destroy completely within me my self-love and, on the other hand, to enkindle in my heart the fire of Your purest love ... (§371) [Jesus responded] "**you will cancel out your will absolutely in this retreat** and, instead, My complete will shall be accomplished in you." [On the following page in her diary a large "X" appears, and these words are seen:] "**From today on, my own will does not exist.**" (§374)

What is described above is exactly what Jesus asks of Luisa and of us all: the total cancellation of our self-will in order that His Divine Will may become the life principle of our souls, just as our souls are the life-principles of our bodies. Clearly, there is little doubt that Jesus revealed the Gift to St. Faustina in her fully approved writings.

Blessed Conchita: The Mystical Incarnation; Much More Than Spiritual Marriage

To Concepción Cabrera de Armida—long known as simply "Venerable Conchita," but now known as *Blessed* Conchita (she was Beatified on May 4th, 2019)—the Gift is revealed in such clarity that no one who reads her writings could fail to see It. She, too, produced thousands of pages of writings, and their **main thrust**[23] **is the same as Luisa's: there is a new sanctity, available for the asking, which far surpasses the greatest possible sanctity of the previous era**. Confirming this analysis, we have the works of Father Marie-Michel Philipon, a Dominican priest and highly esteemed theologian whose works are cited multiple times in the *New Catholic Encyclopedia*. Like St. Hannibal, Fr. Philipon had already proven his authority in discerning alleged private revelations and mystics; long before St. Elizabeth of the Trinity was even declared a Servant of God, Fr. Philipon wrote extensively on her spirituality, and strongly promoted and defended her writings. But he even more strongly endorsed Conchita's revelations, writing a book on them entitled, *Conchita: A Mother's Spiritual Diary*. Towards the end of this work, he sums up Conchita's spirituality, writing:

A theologian must above all pose this question to himself: "What then did God intend to bring about through His humble servant for the benefit of His entire Church?" *The greatest degree of Holiness is attainable for everyone ...* The most sublime mystical graces described by spiritual masters are not privileges confined to souls consecrated to God, priestly and religious life. They are offered to all Christians no matter what their state of life. It seems that God wanted to give us through Conchita living historical proof of this truth. ...The Lord Himself has announced to her that she would be a model wife and mother, but that her mission would extend far beyond to make shine the sanctifying might of Christ and of the Holy Spirit "in all states of life." ... *We are incontestably in a new era of spirituality.*

Fr. Philipon has left no room for doubt or confusion: a new holiness is indeed upon us. It is the *greatest* holiness possible, and it is offered to *all*. Consulting Conchita's revelations directly, we see Fr. Philipon's synthesis confirmed:

My soul empty of all else, I received [Jesus] in Communion ... [Jesus said to me:] "Here I am, I want to incarnate Myself mystically in your heart ...**it is much more than [spiritual marriage; it is, rather] the grace of incarnating Me,** of living and growing in your soul, never to leave it, to possess you and to be possessed by you as in one and the same substance ... in a compenetration which cannot be comprehended: **it is the grace of graces ...It is a union of the same nature as that of the union of heaven, except that in paradise the veil which conceals the Divinity disappears** ... For you [now] keep ever in your soul my real and effective presence."[24]

Recall that to speak of receiving—while still on earth—something "much more" than spiritual marriage (as Jesus does here to Conchita) would never have been accepted in the older works of spiritual theology; and for good reason: there *was not* any such sanctity available for the asking before Luisa received the Gift of Living in the Divine Will in 1889. And yet, Jesus clearly tells Conchita—leaving no possibility of any other interpretation—that He is now giving something much greater than spiritual marriage. This is no tangential remark in Conchita's writings; it is the very purpose of her revelations. Accordingly, the theologian Monsignor Arthur Calkins wrote:

The great crowning grace of her life, received on March 25, 1906, [was] known as the "mystical incarnation." The late Bishop Joseph J. Madera strove to explain this extraordinary grace in this way: "The mystical incarnation may be compared to the indwelling of Jesus in Mary from the moment of His conception in her womb. ... even though God grants extraordinary graces to chosen souls, what he confers on them is eventually intended for the up-building of the entire Body of Christ."[Monsignor Calkins continues:] Although Conchita received this extraordinary grace in 1906, she would effectively spend the rest of her life trying to fathom what had been done in her and how to respond to it.[25]

Blessed Dina Belanger: The State of the Elect in Heaven While on Earth

A Canadian nun who died in 1929 and was beatified along with Blessed Duns Scotus by Pope St. John Paul II in 1993, Blessed Dina received revelations on an extraordinary grace referred to as "Divine Substitution." In his homily at the Beatification Mass, John Paul said she *"actualized in her life celestial gifts that awaken our admiration,"* made specific reference to her *"such high degree of intimacy with God,"* mentioned the *"life of the Most Holy Trinity in her,"* and even singled out for praise her *"desire to correspond fully to the Divine Will."* In Blessed Dina's revelations, Jesus assured her that this new grace He was giving her was so great that she would "not possess me any more completely in Heaven."[26] Within these revelations, Jesus also said:

I wish to deify you in the same manner that I united my Humanity to my Divinity in the Incarnation ...The degree of holiness that I desire for you is my own Holiness, in its infinite plenitude, the Holiness of My Father realized in you by Me.[27] [Dina writes] "This grace which the Trinity of my God grants me with so much love is a foretaste of my participation in the divine life; I say a foretaste, because **it is the state of the elect in heaven, yet I, in bodily form, am still on earth.**[28] [Now] my soul can dwell in heaven, live there without any backward glance toward earth, and yet continue to animate my material being... My union with the Heart of Jesus has been like his real presence after holy communion, while the consecrated Host is still with me."[29]

The spiritual teachings of Blessed Dina are a veritable treasure trove, and what is presented here is only a small fraction of their overlap with Luisa's. But in these quotes alone we see yet another revelation of a new sanctity which is able to bestow **the same holiness that the very saints in Heaven enjoy; one that transforms its recipient into a true living Host; one** that is able to unite the soul to God as the Humanity and Divinity of Christ were united in the Incarnation. It is not possible to even refer to a greater sanctity than this one which is clearly revealed here to this beatified mystic.

St. Elizabeth of the Trinity: Personal Possession of the Trinity

A French Carmelite mystic canonized by Pope Francis in 2016, St. Elizabeth produced writings on the Indwelling of the Trinity which give a solid exposition of the Gift of Living in the Divine Will. Theologian Dr. Anthony Lilles writes:

> When [Elizabeth's] prayer evokes "My God, My Three," **she invites us to take personal possession of the Trinity.** ...She insisted that, in silent stillness before God, the loving gaze of the Father shines within our hearts until God contemplates the likeness of his Son in the soul. ... Such prayer not only sets the soul apart and makes it holy, but it glorifies the Father and even extends the saving work of Christ in the world. She called this "the praise of Glory" and understood this to be her great vocation. By canonizing Elizabeth of the Trinity, the Church has ... validated her mission... (ncregister.com)

Here, too, we see intimations of something new and glorious; **a real sort of personal *possession* of the Trinity. In earlier times, sanctity was only described as a *participation* in the Trinity and nothing more.** Indeed, a response that one sometimes hears after bringing up the heights of sanctity revealed in the Gift is: *"No, we can participate in, but cannot possess, the Divine Nature."* Now, there was nothing wrong with this saying in its day—but the time has now come in which we may indeed, in a real sense, *possess* (only by grace—along with other important distinctions) the Divine Nature as Gift, as this canonized mystic says in her approved writings. Describing her spirituality and most important teachings in greater depth, Hugh Owen writes:

> Elizabeth was asked several questions: "What name would you like to have in Heaven?" "The Will of God," she replied. "What is your motto?" she was asked. "God in me and I in Him," she answered...**Elizabeth believed that the Holy Spirit would transform her into another humanity of Jesus.** She wrote: "O consuming fire! Spirit of love! Descend within me and reproduce within me, as it were, an incarnation of the Word that I may be to him another humanity wherein He renews his mystery! O my Christ...possess me wholly; substitute Thyself for me, that my life may be but a radiance of Thine own...**How can one glorify God? It is not difficult. Our Lord gives us the secret, when he tells us, 'My meat and drink is to do the will of him who sent me'** (John 4:34). ... This is absolute reality, for God is not divided; his will is his whole being..." Interpreting Blessed Elizabeth's spiritual doctrine, Hans Urs Von Balthasar wrote: **"The human will has to be 'enclosed' in the will of God**, for otherwise it remains without focus or direction. [as St. Elizabeth wrote,] 'Our will only becomes free when we enclose it in the will of God'"** ...Through abandonment to the Holy Spirit, Blessed **Elizabeth aspired to be consecrated by Him into a "living host."** She wrote to a priest: "I ask you, as a child its father, to consecrate and sacrifice me in the Holy Mass a host of praise to the glory of God. Consecrate me so well that I may be no longer myself but he, that the Father, looking on me, may recognize him." (*New and Divine*. 74-77)

✱✱✱

And what have we seen thus far? We have seen the Gift being meticulously prepared for over the course of 2,000 years by the Holy Spirit, the *Soul of the Church* (cf. *Catechism* §797) and the Architect of History. We have seen It revealed in utmost clarity to many mystics of the 20th century. We have seen that the primary one to whom Its private revelation has been entrusted, Luisa, is entirely beyond reproach and clearly authentic by any measure. We have seen the whole consensus of prophecy, Papal Magisterium, and the Fathers of the Church trumpeting Its impending Reign over the whole earth. At this point I do not think there are many readers left who still doubt the reality of this Gift or Its Reign. And yet, God, in His extreme desire to miss no opportunity to invite all to believe His words, does not stop there: He also tells us the *"secrets of the history of Creation"* in order to reveal to us why *now* is the perfect time for the Reign's arrival. For it is only fitting that, as God now writes the Dénouement before our eyes, He also in so doing reveal to the very characters within it—that is, you and me—the roles they shall fulfill in the Greatest Story Ever Told.

†‡†

Chapter 4: When Will the Era Arrive?

The answer to this question is very simple: When the Era arrives is up to you. If you want it to arrive very soon, then heed the call presented in Chapter 2, and it may do just that. If you'd prefer that the world limp on in its current state of agony for more years, decades, or even centuries—then simply ignore that call. You yourself may even be the "straw that breaks the camel's back," if only you cast yourself upon that back—which is the present kingdom of the prince of this world: the devil. Jesus was careful to not reveal in His words to Luisa when exactly the Era would come, so as to not mislead anyone into thinking its arrival is a matter of passive waiting. He did, however, say the following:

> I want to make known to you the order of my Providence. **Every course of two thousand years I have renewed the world. In the first two thousand years I renewed it with the Flood; in the second two thousand I renewed it with my coming upon earth ... Now we are at the turn of the third two thousand years,** and there will be a third renewal. This is the reason for the general confusion—it is nothing other than the preparation for the third renewal ... in this third renewal, after the earth has been purged and the current generation destroyed for the most part, I will be even more generous with creatures. (January 29, 1919)

Since Jesus here essentially promised the Era would come "about" 2,000 years after Redemption, it will indeed do just that. Jesus—God—knows everything, including every single detail of the entire future (human free will does not change this fact), and He never lies. He also does not exaggerate. But He does *round,* for everybody rounds; it is necessary and there is nothing dishonest about it. No one, in giving directions to another, says "take a right after 5,376.5 feet;" rather, he says "take a right in a mile,"—even though a mile is 5,280 feet—and one who takes a right-hand turn after exactly 5,280 feet and consequently drives into a ditch has only himself to blame. The only thing, therefore, that we can say with certainty about the arrival of the Era is that it will occur by such a time that it would not be an erroneous rounding to say it is "about" 2,000 years after Redemption. Of course, that does not say much, and countless signs of the times seem to make it clear that the long-prophesied events which will precede the Era are at the very doorstep, not 400 years away. And although we have settled that the Era does not need to come *exactly* two thousand years after Redemption (2026 A.D., 2033 A.D., or somewhere in between, depending upon whose scholarship is correct), there is no denying that such a time of arrival would be very fitting, and perhaps if all who read these words truly devote themselves to hastening the coming of the Kingdom, such a fitting fulfillment will become a reality.

Let us do more, however, than just be satisfied with knowing that now is the time—let us see why, in accordance with 6,000 years of God's arduous preparation for this moment, now is the *perfect* time for the completion of *His Story*.

The Story of History: Redux

We began this book by considering the Story of History primarily under the aspect of simple reason. Now, let us consider the same Story, and learn from that which—although it both works with reason and requires it—is nevertheless far superior: *Faith*. As Jesus tells Luisa, **"If you remain attentive to live always of my Will, It will entrust to you all the secrets of the history of Creation."** (August 22, 1931) We will again start at the very beginning in our endeavor to discover these secrets God wishes to share with us.

The Original Glory and the Fall

The Universe does predate man chronologically, but ontologically it takes a low second place. "The purpose of Creation was man, yet I did not create man as first; had I done it I would not have been orderly." (November 20, 1929) And what relation was man's creation directed toward with respect to these material things that were made for his sake? **"Creation was made for man—in it he was to be the king of all created things."** (July 29, 1926) So, God made creation for man, and He made man to be its king. And this, indeed, Adam was upon his creation. For it was only just for man to be creation's king, in accordance with the incredible dignity that man was given. Jesus tells Luisa that He made physical creation to house man, *but He made the soul of man to house God.* This was so deeply true that the Divine Will was *the very principle of the life* and action of Adam—a truth also attested to by the Fathers of the Church. Jesus tells Luisa that Adam "possessed such sanctity that the slightest one of his acts had such value that no [sanctity of any] saint either before or after My coming to earth can compare to his sanctity." (October 2, 1927) But everyone must be tried; no creature with a free will is exempt from a test before absolute confirmation in grace. Even though we know what transpired—and God knew what would transpire before it did—it would nevertheless be blasphemous to accuse God of so testing Adam and Eve without His ordained Will being that they pass the test. And He knew exactly what to do if they passed. Jesus tells Luisa:

> If Adam had passed the test, all human generations would have been confirmed in his state of happiness and of royalty. (April 1, 1928) **If Adam had not sinned, the Eternal Word, who is the very Will of the Celestial Father, was to come upon earth glorious, triumphant and dominator, accompanied visibly by His angelic army, which all were to see;** and with the splendor of His glory, He was to charm everyone and draw everyone to Himself with His beauty; crowned as king and with the scepter of command, so as to be king and head of the human family, in such a way as to give creatures the great honor of being able to say: 'We have a King who is Man and God.' (March 31, 1929)

What a glorious plan! With so great a plan in mind why, then, did God allow the Fall? For it is inadequate to pretend that appealing to Adam's free will fully explains the matter—God only so much as *allows* any evil whatsoever to occur if strict conditions are met: He must know a good will come of it, it must be a *greater* good than the permitted evil, and there must be no other way. The *felix culpa* (the "happy fault" of Adam), of which we sing in the Exsultet at Easter, and in which we remember that in a sense Adam's fault was "happy," speaks to this reality. For after the Fall, God was on the move to enact an even *greater* plan than He would have enacted if Adam had passed the test. But how is this plan greater if the plan itself can be said to be the restoration of what was lost at the Fall? The answer is that this new plan *entails* such a restoration, but *does not consist merely in* this restoration. God did not delay in enacting His new plan:

> Terrible indeed was the moment of the fall of Adam. As he rejected Our Divine Will to do his own, Our Fiat was in act of withdrawing from the heavens, from the sun and from all Creation to reduce It to nothing ... **If it wasn't that the Eternal Word offered His foreseen merits of the future Redeemer, as He offered them to preserve the Immaculate Virgin from original sin, everything would have gone to ruin**: the heavens, the sun, would have withdrawn... (October 7, 1929)

The Protoevangelium. Yes, the Fall of Man was so great that, were it not for the foreseen merits of the incarnate Christ, the Universe would have been annihilated; resolving into the chaos whence it was called by God in the beginning. So greatly exalted is man's dignity above created things that their destiny is inextricably linked to his own. But God's infinite mercy did not delay: **"I will put enmities between thee and the woman, and thy seed and her seed: she shall crush thy head, and thou shalt lie in wait for her heel."**–Genesis 3:15. Expounding upon this, Jesus tells Luisa:

> My daughter, my Love was not extinguished because of the fall of man, but became more ignited; and even though my Justice justly punished him and condemned him, my Love, kissing my Justice, without delay promised the future Redeemer, and said to the deceitful serpent, with the empire of my Power: 'You have made use of a woman to snatch man from my Divine Will, and I, by means of another woman, who will have in Her power the Power of my Fiat, will knock down your pride, and with Her immaculate foot, She will crush your head.' These words burned the infernal serpent more than hell itself. (May 19, 1931)

As soon as the Fall had occurred, God was on the move not only to restore what was lost, but to reorder things in a greater way than would have been possible if the Fall had never occurred. Now we can understand why the Fall was allowed and why the essence of the Third Fiat does not stand in contrast to Christian holiness, which is already in some ways superior to Adam's prelapsarian holiness. God, indeed, created Adam with the highest category of holiness. In accordance with what we discussed in the beginning of Chapter 2, it is clear that to claim God did not do so would be to blaspheme His Goodness by claiming He created a being without its due perfection.

God permitted Adam to fall because He foresaw a coming age in which Adam's highest category of holiness could be combined with Christian grace through the merits of the Incarnation and Passion of His Son. In that coming age, treasures could be built up in Heaven that could not possibly have existed without the Fall—treasures that will make the blood, sweat, and tears of their attainment seem like nothing. These treasures embellish our eternal home, Heaven. Were Adam to have never fallen, although we would never have lost the terrestrial paradise and the perfect state of our souls, the celestial paradise would not have received the same glorifications, and we would be eternally devoid of the crowns which we now have the ability to merit if we so choose. These glorious crowns proceed from our willing suffering and our participation in the Passion of the Incarnate Christ; which in turn could not have happened without a fall, as Christ would then have had no cause to suffer. Without the Passion of Christ, God's infinite love for us also would never have had its most perfect and beautiful exposition. Therefore we can indeed say that, "thanks to" the fall of Adam, we will have the most glorious possible and imaginable exposition of Divine Love before our eyes for all eternity in the marks that Our Lord continues to carry in His hands, feet, and side—even in Heaven. Indeed, when one carefully observes this *Greatest Story Ever Told*, it becomes clear that there is no contradiction between—on the one hand—God's ultimate plan entailing the restoration of what was lost at the Fall and—on the other hand—Christian holiness being in a sense greater than original holiness. In fact, **only now that Jesus has revealed this ultimate plan in detail to Luisa do mysteries which have hitherto perplexed the greatest minds throughout the history of the Church begin to become unveiled.** Explaining this dynamic far better than my own feeble words can, Jesus tells Luisa:

> My daughter, I created the creature beautiful, noble, with eternal and divine origin, full of happiness and worthy of Me. Sin ruined him from top to bottom, it disennobled him, it deformed him, and rendered him the most unhappy creature… Now, my Redemption ransomed the creature from sin, and my Humanity acted just like a tender mother with her newborn…And with my wounds I covered their deformities, rendering them *more beautiful than before*; and if in creating them I made them like clearest and noble heavens, in Redemption I adorned them, studding them with the most refulgent stars of my wounds so as to cover their ugliness and render them more beautiful. To their wounds and deformities I attached the diamonds, the pearls, the gems of my pains in order to hide all their evils and clothe them with such magnificence as to surpass the state of their origin. This is why, with reason, the Church says: 'Happy fault'—because with sin came Redemption; and my Humanity not only nourished them with Its Blood, but clothed them with Its own Person, and adorned them with Its own beauty. (February 26, 1922)

Returning to our chronological adventure through the Story of History, we see that the world was not ready to immediately receive the fulfillment of God's plan—though indeed it was now a sure promise. Rather, another 6,000 years of suffering and praying—4,000 for the coming of the Redeemer, then 2,000 for the coming of His Kingdom—would first have to pass.

Up to Redemption

Despite the Fall, the world did not immediately descend into great evil. Jesus tells Luisa:

> Even though Adam did not speak extensively about the Kingdom of my Will, he taught many important things on what regarded It; so much so, that during the first times of the history of the world, up to Noah, the generations had no need of laws, nor were there idolatries … but all recognized their one God … because they cared more about my Will. But as they kept moving away from It, idolatries arose and degenerated into worse evils. (September 17, 1926)

Although the Edenic graces were removed upon the Fall, its effects lingered for some time, and Adam carried many graces with him still. But as time went on, and as centuries passed after the death of Adam, the world grew farther away from its noble origin. Thankfully, there was at least still one righteous man left. Jesus tells Luisa:

> In the [time of] the Flood … only Noah, by obeying Our Will and through the prolixity of his long sacrifice of building the ark, deserved to be saved with his family, and to find in his acts the continuation of the long generation in which the promised Messiah was to come. (March 12, 1930)

With the world now purged and essentially beginning again, God was able to set to work much more rapidly with His plan. He made His covenant with Abraham, formed His people Israel in Egypt, brought them out through Moses and gave them The Law, and

then, the closer the time came to the ultimate Divine Intervention in the Incarnation, the more prophets He sent to prepare the way and stir up the needed longing, expectation, and prayer of the people. This great increase in prophecy, proportional in intensity to the proximity of the time of the incarnation, has not been lost on modern scholars, who have pointed out that even recent archeological manuscript discoveries have shown that "a great ferment and fervor existed in the period just before the beginning of Christianity."[30] And this prophetic explosion was not in vain; it culminated in the unprecedented glories of a certain lowly virgin named Mary. Jesus tells Luisa:

> So, in the Old Testament, the more I multiplied the good, the patriarchs and the prophets, the more pressing were the invitations and the mail that ran between Heaven and earth, through which God was sending news—that He desired the new union. This is so true that, unable to contain the ardor of His love any longer, and since decayed humanity was not yet disposed at that time, He made an exception, espousing the Virgin Queen and the Humanity of the Word with bond of true marriage, so that, by virtue of them, decayed humanity might be lifted up again and I might form the marriage with the entire humanity. (June 16, 1928)

Now the fullness of time has come. Now the hour has arrived for God to fulfill His promise He made 4,000 years earlier. And where does it all begin? In the womb.

> My conception in the womb of a Virgin was the greatest work of the whole history of the world. ... Heaven and earth are still astounded and enraptured, and all felt invaded by so much love as to be able to feel my Life conceived within all. (September 28, 1935)

In the Annunciation—the Incarnation of the Word—that which is scarcely even possible to imagine did, in fact, transpire in reality. The Infinite entered into the finite. The Creator entered into His own creation. The One Who made the Universe became a child in the womb of a creature within the Universe. God and man were no longer foreign to each other; for there was now a God-man Who would proceed to call all His children into Himself. Finally, after 4,000 long years, the Divine Will had its place of reigning: the home of Nazareth. But He did not yet have His Kingdom. Jesus tells Luisa:

> My daughter, indeed my Divine Will reigned in this house of Nazareth on earth as It does in Heaven. ... But I was like a king without a people... therefore I cannot say that, on coming upon earth, I had the Kingdom of my Fiat at that time. Our Kingdom was for Us only, because the order of Creation, the royalty of man, was not restored. However, by the Celestial Mother and I living wholly of Divine Will, the seed was sown, the yeast was formed, so as to make Our Kingdom arise and grow upon earth. Therefore, all the preparations were made, all the graces impetrated, all the pains suffered, so that the Kingdom of my Fiat might come to reign upon earth. **This is why Nazareth can be called the point of recall of the Kingdom of Our Will.** (July 7, 1928)

In Nazareth, there was the point of recall of the Kingdom. The work had begun; so much, however, was left to be done; for Jesus of Nazareth would have to leave His home in order to preach the Kingdom. Sadly, upon the commencement of His public ministry, the learned largely wanted nothing to do with Jesus. Those who should have been first to recognize Him and worship Him were the very ones to reject Him. (Jesus even acknowledged this in the context of telling Luisa that His revelations to her today are treated just as He was 2,000 years ago, lamenting: "No learned man followed Me, but [only the] poor, ignorant and simple." (February 24, 1933)) In fact, far from merely failing to follow Him, they conspired against Him and crucified their own God.

Redemption and the Church

"When I am lifted up from the earth, I will draw all men to myself." (John 12:32) It was by this Crucifixion that Christ won the salvation of the world. **As He hung on the cross, the Church was born from His own Sacred Side, which gushed forth blood and water as a "fountain of mercy for us." This Church was destined to serve as the New Ark for the whole world, even unto the end of time.** With the incarnation, passion, death, and resurrection of Jesus, and the institution of the Sacraments, the evils that had multiplied and grown for thousands of years began to diminish. The Gospel spread throughout the world, and with its proclamation came the transformation of entire nations, as well as individual lives, and everything in between.

Meanwhile, something amazing was happening; something unnoticed by history books, but which was truly unprecedented and far outshining all the grand events depicted within their pages—God began preparing the way for the Gift He would in time bestow upon the world. These preparations consisted in a sanctity that flourished and grew in the inner life of the Church in the *Four Paradigms* we discussed in the last Chapter. Since we have already covered that development, however, we will presently move on to consider the next stage in the Story of History: the Kingdom (even while acknowledging that Church History, glorious as it is, deserves a much lengthier treatment than we are here giving it!). Although, with the Incarnation, the Kingdom has already come in an important sense, and in another sense will only receive its *definitive perfection* in Heaven, there is another important sense in which the Kingdom still shall come more fully on earth—the sense relayed in the primary petition of the *Our Father* prayer, faithfully recited billions of times each day by the Church. For, indeed, **the fruits of Christianity are astounding— but they have not yet attained their full intent, which is to conclusively and exhaustively call down the Kingdom upon earth. No one can deny that God's Will does not yet reign upon earth as fully as it should.** *But two thousand years' worth of effort will not go unrewarded.* Jesus tells Luisa:

> My daughter, when Adam sinned God gave him the promise of the future Redeemer. Centuries passed and the promise did not fail, therefore human generations enjoyed the blessings of the Redemption. Now, by My coming from heaven to form the Kingdom of Redemption, I made another more solemn promise before departing for heaven: The Kingdom of My Will on earth, which is contained in the 'Our Father' prayer… So after I formed this prayer in the presence of My heavenly Father, certain that he would grant Me the Kingdom of My Divine Will on earth, I taught it to My apostles so that they might teach it to the whole world, and that one might be the cry of all: 'Your Will be done on earth as it is in heaven.' A promise more sure and solemn I could not make … **souls must await it with the same certainty with which they awaited the future Redeemer.** For My Divine Will is bound and committed to the words of the 'Our Father.' And when My Divine Will binds itself, whatever it promises is more than certain to come to pass. (February 5, 1928)

It is this Third Fiat that He now ardently desires to give to the world, but He is waiting for our response. He is waiting for us to strive sufficiently for it, pray for it, and yearn for it. He is waiting for us to live in His Will even now, and perform as many acts in His Will as we can, in order to prepare the ground for Its universal Reign. He is waiting for us to sufficiently spread knowledge of the Kingdom of His Will before He can institute Its true triumph. We must remember that "the greatest story ever told" is not over and done with just because the Apostle John has already died and the Deposit of Faith is sealed! Public revelation is indeed already complete, but that does not mean God is now simply waiting for the time to come to put an end to our misery and commence the consummation of the world and is otherwise finished with His interventions. Far from it, as Jesus tells Luisa:

> [The two] links connected together-the Redemption and the Kingdom of My Divine Will [are] inseparable from each other. The Redemption was to prepare, suffer, do; the Kingdom of the Fiat was to fulfill and possess-both of them of highest importance. (December 25, 1927)

On the contrary, far from being over, this Great Story is nearing its fulfillment in the coming of the Kingdom. As we discussed in this book's first pages, we are now in the Dénouement, and this fact has become completely undeniable, considering the Prophetic Explosion of the 20th Century which we will consider in the next pages. First, though, we will consider the following passages of Luisa's writings, in which Jesus' own words make clear that we are indeed precisely at this moment:

> There is much analogy between the way in which Redemption unfolded and the way in which the Kingdom of my Divine Will will unfold. See, in my Redemption I chose a Virgin, in appearance She had no importance according to the world...I chose Her from Nazareth, [but] I wanted for it to belong to the capital city, Jerusalem, in which there was the body of the pontiffs and priests who then represented Me ... For the Kingdom of my Divine Will I have chosen another virgin who, in appearance, has no importance... the very city of Corato [Luisa's hometown in Italy] is not an important city, but it belongs to Rome, in which resides my representative on earth, the Roman Pontiff, from whom come my divine laws; and just as he makes it his duty to make my Redemption known to the peoples, so will he make it his duty to make known the Kingdom of my Divine Will. It can be said that one and the other will proceed in the same way. (January 30, 1930) In the Redemption, every Manifestation that was made by Us about the descent of the Word on earth, was one step that We made toward mankind. And **as they yearned and prayed for It, and Our Manifestations, Prophecies, and Revelations, were manifested to the people ... as the time of having to descend from Heaven to earth drew near, so We increased the Prophets** ... (May 30, 1932)

What is it that we see here? An incredible symmetry; for, as it is often said, "even if history does not repeat itself, it does rhyme." Luisa was indeed a sinner like any of us. She was an ordinary Italian laywoman—not the Immaculate Queen of the Universe like Our Lady! And yet, who can fail to see the truth in the parallels described by Jesus above? Who can fail to see how Providentially these events have been orchestrated? Our Lady remains the Queen of this mission, and the one creature who desires the coming of the Kingdom far more than any other. **Furthermore, among all of her many titles, she has inspired one surprising title to suddenly rise to the top in popular devotion just in the last few years: *Our Lady, Undoer of Knots*. This, too, is anything but accidental. The very etymology of the word *Dénouement* comes from the French and Latin words for "untying the knot." The Immaculate Queen is about to undo the knot that was tied in the Garden.**

But even those who cannot see the perfect fittingness of Jesus' action in Luisa's soul and in her writings will certainly not fail to see the explosion of private revelation that Heaven has blessed this world with in the last century, and how this explosion precisely mirrors the increase of Prophets before the Redemption itself.

The Prophetic Explosion of the Modern Era

More than any other century, the last one stands out in the history of the Church. Heaven has been pounding us with incessant pleas for our attention regarding what is about to come (a few of these pleas were covered in Chapter I). It has reached the point that no one who looks at what is happening can dismiss it. Although some today, lamentably, try to pretend that all is business as usual and there is nothing particularly special about the age in which we live (as far as Heaven's intervention is concerned), even the secular world has not failed to take notice that something consequential is happening. *National Geographic* ran a lengthy article in 2015 on this worldwide explosion of apparitions, showing their exponential increase in the 1900s. Bolstering this analysis, the late theologian, Fr. Edward O'Connor, wrote in his book entitled *Listen to my Prophets*:

> [Apparitions] of the Blessed Virgin Mary are being reported far more frequently than at any time in the past. ...there were very few during the first ten centuries. After that they increased moderately, reaching 105 in the nineteenth century. But during the twentieth century ... [there were reported] a total of 1,045 apparitions of the Blessed Mother ... (Introduction IX)

In the same book, Fr. O'Connor spends hundreds of pages analyzing dozens of the most important revelations, messages, apparitions, and locutions of the modern Era, and says the following about their prophetic consensus:

> The basic message is that of St. Faustina: we are in an age of mercy, which will soon give way to an age of justice. The reason for this is the immorality of today's world, which surpasses that of any past age. ...God has been sending prophets as never before to call us to repentance. Most often, it is the Blessed Mother who speaks through them. She warns of an unprecedented tribulation that lies in the very near future. The Church will be torn apart. The Antichrist, already alive in the world, will manifest himself. ... Not only the Church, but the whole world will experience tribulation. There will be natural disasters, such as earthquakes, floods, fierce storms and strange weather patterns. Economic ruin will plunge the whole world into poverty. There will be warfare, perhaps even a Third World War. There will also be cosmic disasters in the form of devastating meteors striking the earth or other heavenly bodies passing close enough to wreak havoc. Finally, a mysterious fire from heaven will wipe out the greater part of mankind, and plunge the world in utter darkness for three days. Before these terrible events take place, **we will be prepared, first by a "Warning" in which everyone on earth will see his or her soul as it appears before God,** and secondly by a miraculous sign. **The disasters to come will purify the world and leave it as God intended it to be. The Holy Spirit will be poured out as never before and renew the hearts of all mankind. Most of the visionaries insist that the time left before these things take place is very short.** (189-190)

Now, some of the revelations may wind up being condemned or even proven false. But this changes nothing. *All* of them would have to be proven false—which will never happen—for their consensus to be doubtful. **And their consensus is this: the end of this sad era is fast approaching. The events spoken of in the Book of Revelation are about to begin (enormous Chastisements, followed by a glorious Era in which Christ reigns in grace). These events cannot be averted, but the Chastisements can be mitigated and shortened, and the Era can be hastened, and above all, the salvation and sanctification of souls can be achieved more powerfully than ever in the midst of these events—by the prayer and action of the Faithful who must devote themselves wholeheartedly to this task.** I do not want to even attempt to give a cursory overview of individual private revelations here; I will leave that task to the research of each reader and I exhort its undertaking. This research will be enormously edifying and eye-opening, and I especially recommend the works of Mark Mallett, Fr. Joseph Iannuzzi, and Fr. Edward O'Connor.

And so, instead of reviewing the specifics here, suffice it to say that we are living in unprecedented times. Heaven is on the move like never before. *This means something.* And it means this: the Kingdom of God is at hand. But the devil is also aware of what is happening, and he will not miss his opportunity to strike. As Scripture says: "The serpent poured water like a river out of his mouth after the woman, to sweep her away with the flood." (Revelation 12:15) This is precisely what we see today in the flood of false apparitions, revelations, mystics, etc. that have done so much damage. We should not be surprised that this is happening. The devil always apes the things of God. As followers of Christ, we must have the courage to trust that God will give us the grace to discern the difference between the Good Shepherd (Whose voice we know) and the "liar and murderer from the beginning." (John 8:44) Rejecting this trust means closing our ears to Heaven, which is far too great a price to pay merely for the supposed "safety" of not succumbing to a trap set by the devil. Pray, discern, obey the decisions of the Church when she definitively renders them, look for the fruits, never contradict orthodoxy as laid out in the Catechism, and remain in a state of grace and close to the Sacraments; thus, you can proceed with great confidence when it comes to private revelation, even if not yet fully approved (more on this point is found in the appendices). **When you do this—that is, keep open your eyes, ears, hearts, and minds to the calls of Heaven—you will quickly and easily realize, even outside of Luisa's revelations, that The Story of History has now approached the Time of the Coronation, its own Dénouement, by way of the arrival of the Crown of Sanctity.**

The Time for the Coronation

We are still in the Age of the Church—we always will be until the end of time. But we have now arrived at the moment when the Church is almost ready for her crown; the moment when the prayer she has been praying more fervently than all others—that is, the *Our Father*—is ready to be fulfilled. But, as many triumphs as the Church has seen—and there have been so many glorious ones that they are almost difficult to believe—the common temptation is nevertheless one of despairing of her Coronation ever coming; a temptation Luisa herself voiced when she said:

> How can this Kingdom of the Divine Will ever come? Sin abounds, evil worsens... [Jesus responds to Luisa's lamentation:] My daughter, everything is possible to us. Impossibilities, difficulties, insurmountable cliffs of creatures melt before our Supreme Majesty, as snow now opposite to an ardent Sun...Didn't it happen thus in the Redemption? Sin abounded more than ever, (there was) hardly a little nucleus of people that longed for the Messiah, and in the midst of this nucleus how many hypocrisies, how many sins of all kinds, often idolatry. But it was decreed that I should come upon the earth. **Before our decrees all the evils cannot impede that which we want to do...Now as my coming upon the earth was our decree, thus is decreed our Kingdom of our Will upon the earth. Rather it can be said that the one and the other are one single decree, [and] that having completed the first act of this decree, there remains the second to complete**...It is true that the times are sad, the people themselves are tired. They see all the ways closed ... But this doesn't impede that the Kingdom of my Supreme Fiat comes... (January 3, 1932)

The coming of the Kingdom is a guarantee. Nothing and no one can stop it. It is going to come: the only question is when, and on which side of its coming will we choose to stand? Because **what must precede it is coming like a freight train, and it is not something you want to be on the wrong side of. Our Lord was not shy in revealing to Luisa that this Coronation of Creation will be preceded by great Chastisements.** He said to her:

> Do you think that things will always be as they are today? Ah! no. My Will will overwhelm everything; It will cause confusion everywhere—all things will be turned upside down. Many new phenomena will occur, such as to confound the pride of man; wars, revolutions, casualties of every kind will not be spared, in order to knock man down, and to dispose him to receive the regeneration of the Divine Will in the human will. And everything I manifest to you about my Will, as well as everything you do in It, is nothing other than preparing the way, the means, the teachings, the light, the graces, so that my Will may be regenerated in the human will… (June 18, 1925) My daughter, [the Chastisements] will serve to purify and prepare the human family. The turmoils will serve to reorder, and the destructions to build more beautiful things. If a collapsing building is not torn down, a new and more beautiful one cannot be formed upon those very ruins. I will stir everything for the fulfillment of my Divine Will. …[Redemption] has not yet covered all of Its way; many regions and peoples live as if I had not come, therefore it is necessary that It make Its way and walk everywhere, because Redemption is the preparatory way for the Kingdom of My Will… And when We decree, all is done… what seems difficult to you will all be made easy by Our Power. (April 30, 1928)

As the life of the Church must follow the life of her Head; that is, Christ Himself, she too will have a time in her history that corresponds to His passion, and also a time that corresponds to the period of His resurrected presence on earth (the Era of Peace; the Reign of the Divine Will) before His Ascension into Heaven (which, in turn, corresponds to the End of Time and the Church's definitive perfection in the Heavenly Wedding Feast; this order is precisely the description Jesus uses with Luisa—that the saints of the past centuries symbolize Jesus' Humanity, but the saints of the new Era will symbolize His Resurrection (cf. April 15, 1919).) **But we must understand that the Chastisements do not detract one iota from the love that God has for all of us**, for the Chastisements themselves are actually great acts of Divine Love. Jesus tells Luisa:

> My daughter, courage, everything will serve for the triumph of my Will. If I strike, it is because I want to restore… You must know that **I always love my children, my beloved creatures, I would turn Myself inside out so as not to see them struck;** so much so, that in the gloomy times that are coming, I have placed them all in the hands of my Celestial Mama—to Her have I entrusted them, that She may keep them for Me under Her safe mantle. I will give Her all those whom She will want; even death will have no power over those who will be in the custody of my Mama. [Luisa then relates:] Now, while He was saying this, my dear Jesus showed me, with facts, how the Sovereign Queen descended from Heaven with an unspeakable majesty, and a tenderness fully maternal; and She went around in the midst of creatures, throughout all nations, and She marked Her dear children and those who were not to be touched by the scourges. (June 6, 1935)

What profound words. Jesus tells us that *He would turn Himself inside out* (another translation says that He would *eviscerate* Himself) in order to not see any of us—His dear children—harmed by Chastisements. No one comes even close to Jesus in utterly despising the thought of Chastisements and lamenting their impending arrival. He only allows them—it would not even usually be correct to say that He "imposes" or "sends" them, as most Chastisements are a natural result of mankind's sinfulness—as an utter last resort to save us from the fires of hell, and because He sees the glory that will follow them: **"If [Our Will] supports and tolerates so much, it is because We see the times to** come, Our Purpose Realized." (May 30, 1932) In this same diary entry, we also see Luisa describing how she saw in the Queen of Heaven, Our Blessed Lady, the sure protection from all Chastisements for her dear children. Let us, therefore, especially remember Our Lady's power over all things which are to transpire on this world in the sad days to come before the glorious ones thereafter. And whenever we are tempted to fear, let us instead re-consecrate ourselves to her and renew our love of and devotion to her—fulfilling her requests at Fatima for the daily Rosary and First Saturday devotion and elsewhere for the proclamation of the Fifth Marian Dogma and a life centered on prayer, the Eucharist, Confession, fasting, and Scripture.

Nevertheless, the Chastisements remain necessary. Jesus would have far preferred to conquer this world for Himself and so institute His Kingdom upon it by virtue of love and by way of the graces working through the dissemination of the knowledges He revealed to Luisa. But man has spurned Him thus far. Because of this response of man to God's initiative, there is simply no other possible scenario for the course of the future than the Chastisements (notwithstanding our ability to mitigate them). The Chastisements, indeed, are guaranteed to do the job. They are not how God wanted it to happen, but they will work. In her diary, Luisa observes:

> The cause of [these chastisements] is only sin, and man does not want to surrender; it seems that man has placed himself against God, and God will arm the elements against man—water, fire, wind and many other things, which will cause many upon many to die. (April 17, 1906)

Similarly, Jesus reveals to Luisa:

> Tired of an agony of centuries, my Will wants to get out, and therefore It prepares two ways: the triumphant way, which are Its knowledges, Its prodigies and all the good that the Kingdom of the Supreme Fiat will bring; and the way of Justice, for those who do not want to know It as triumphant. *It is up to the creatures to choose the way in which they want to receive It.* (November 19, 1926)

The Chastisements **will be proportional in duration, scope, and severity to the deficiency of the knowledges of the Divine Will among the people** (a clear corollary of what Jesus says above). **Do you want, then, to mitigate the Chastisements? Do you want to spare this world some of the historically unprecedented misery that is about to deluge it? Be a New Evangelist of the Third Fiat. Proclaim the Kingdom. Proclaim the Divine Mercy while we still have the benefit of the Time of Mercy, which is so quickly drawing to a close.** Recall also that one who lives in the Divine Will—and truly, any soul in God's grace— has no fear of the Chastisements (even though he urgently desires to mitigate them for the sake of his brothers and sisters), for even at their most terrible, he approaches the Chastisements like a person with dirt on his body approaches a shower. Jesus tells Luisa:

> Courage is of souls resolute to do good. They are imperturbable under any storm; and while they hear the roaring of the thunders and lightnings to the point of trembling, and remain under the pouring rain that pours over them, **they use the water to be washed and come out more beautiful; and *heedless of the storm*, they are more than ever resolute and courageous** …courage is the bread of the strong, courage is the warlike one that knows how to win any battle. (April 16, 1931)

And because it is the Chastisements that are the most imminent of all the events we have spoken of within this book's pages, it is with these words that I will conclude the corpus of this book. But I repeat that the details of their duration, severity, and scope are not set in stone; they can be dramatically reduced by our zealous and wholehearted efforts to hasten the Era. As I write these words I am literally on my knees on concrete, begging you to do so—begging you to stop sinning and be converted (sin will only render the Chastisements more severe), begging you to trust in the Divine Mercy (which you will need for enduring the Chastisements), begging you to Live in and Proclaim the Divine Will (which will mitigate the Chastisements and hasten the Era)—listening, as I currently am, to the beautiful chirping of birds and enjoying the golden beams of sunlight that at this moment grace my home after a great thunderstorm has just passed much more quickly than the forecasters said it would, and without causing any of the damage that they cautioned those in my neighborhood to expect. It is not too late to make it so with the whole world.

†‡†

Appendices

Living in the Divine Will Cheat Sheet

Strive to be in continuous conversation with Jesus: all day, every day. Constantly pray "Jesus, I Trust in You," "Thy Will be Done," and "Thy Kingdom Come." Continually thank Him for everything. ·· **Strive to do everything as an Act in the Divine Will** by asking that Jesus do whatever you are doing in you, and ensuring that your **every** act is pure love. ·· **Ask God for the Gift of Living in the Divine Will every day.** ·· **Grow in virtue every day. Live the beatitudes.** *Be a saint!* ·· **Spread knowledge of the Divine Will!** The time of the coming of the Kingdom depends largely upon your zealous dissemination of this knowledge. ·· **Consecrate yourself to Mary** using St. Louis de Montfort's 33-day approach and live out your Consecration totally. ·· **Pray the Rosary every day** and pray it as a family. Pray from the heart; let this prayer become your *joy.* Keep Rosary beads always on hand. ·· **Wear a Crucifix, Miraculous Medal, and Brown Scapular.** ·· Gently, gracefully, and naturally **evangelize in every conversation;** even if you are only subtly sowing a very small seed. ·· **Attend Mass and receive Communion daily** if you can. ·· **Pray the Divine Mercy Chaplet every day** and live the Divine Mercy revelations given to St. Faustina. ·· **Go to confession at least once a month.** ·· **Never waste suffering. Love every cross God sends you,** and bear it with resignation, abnegation, patience, peace, and joy. Never fail to at least say "Jesus, I offer this to You" in every single pain, discomfort, displeasure, disappointment, temptation, etc. ·· **Make sure you are doing regular works of mercy.** ·· **Do a daily or weekly Holy Hour at your nearest Adoration Chapel.** ·· **Try to set aside at least 15 minutes a day for mental prayer:** time you dedicate solely to striving after meditation, contemplation, and the Rounds. ·· **Do spiritual reading every day: Scripture, Magisterium,** Luisa's revelations, saint biographies and writings, the Liturgy of the Hours (Divine Office), etc. ·· **Fast each Wednesday and Friday as you deem yourself called** in accordance with your particular needs and abilities. ·· **Ensure that your home is a holy place** conducive to the spiritual growth of all its members. The Kingdom will come one Nazareth at a time. Imitate the example of the Holy Family, consecrate your family to them, and pray daily for their intercession.

Miscellaneous Resources

- Luisa's Writings: become associated with an existing Divine Will group so that the Volumes may licitly be shared with you. There are many such groups online.
- The Benedictines of the Divine Will: www.benedictinesofdivinewill.org. There you can find the full text of the *Hours of the Passion*, the *Blessed Virgin Mary in the Kingdom of the Divine Will*, Luisa's Letters, and many other materials.
- The official website for Luisa's cause: www.luisapiccarretaofficial.org.
- Fr. Iannuzzi's website on Living in the Divine Will: www.ltdw.org.
- A great website on the Divine Will: www.comingofthekingdom.org.
- Fr. Robert Young's talks on the Divine Will: www.divinewilllife.org.

Concerns of Catholics Addressed

This section will be brief. Whoever is looking for better answers to these or other concerns should consult pages 488 to 532 of *The Crown of Sanctity* (or, for concerns related to Millenarianism and the Era, pages 356-396). Far more important, however, than feeling that all of one's concerns have been satisfactorily addressed, is recognizing and remembering what we covered in Chapter I: given the extraordinary amount of approvals, validations, endorsements, miracles, etc., that Luisa's life, writings, and cause have enjoyed; there is little room to doubt her revelations are anything but Heaven sent.

Now, Luisa's writings are thousands of pages long; dive into them, and you likely will stumble upon some things that perplex (and maybe even annoy!) you at first. Worry not. Set the perplexities aside and come back to them later. This is how we must *always* proceed with mysticism of such magnitude, instead of supposing that embarking upon a new adventure ought to be nothing more than a confirmation of all our pre-existing fancies, preferences, opinions, and in-need-of-growth personal understandings. The absence of any such difficulties in a text is a sure sign that it originated, not from Heaven (which always has loftier aims than confirming the status-quo), but perhaps from a corporate public-relations marketing firm that was hired for its expertise in being inoffensive.

Isn't this just a private revelation that I may ignore if I wish?

Jesus' revelations to Luisa are indeed "just" private revelations—along with Fatima, Guadalupe, Divine Mercy, the Sacred Heart, etc. A revelation being "merely" private neither diminishes its glory nor thereby grants blanket permission to Catholics to licitly reject it on the sole grounds that it is "only private." Let us never forget that the Rosary, too, is a *private* revelation; one about which the Servant of God Sr. Lucia of Fatima rightly said, "**All** people of good will can, and **must** say the Rosary every day."[31]

For it is not true to say that private revelation can never lay any moral claims upon the consciences of Catholics. Like all lies, it is built upon a legitimate premise: that private revelation does not bind *as a matter* of *supernatural Catholic Faith.* But it fallaciously asserts that merely because a given matter is not an explicit constituent of Public Revelation's *Depositum Fidei*, no Catholic can ever have any obligation *of any sort* in the matter. Although promoted vociferously by a few, this idea is in stark contrast to the reality that **you and God both know what invitations He has extended to your heart, and on Judgment Day your eternal glory will be meted out by how you responded to these Divine Invitations, and not just by whether you had faith in the contents of the Deposit**

of Faith.

The latter standard would be little more than a Catholicized version of the old "Faith Alone" heresy, which is finally being abandoned even by many Protestants. This heresy essentially holds that the only question in salvation is whether one believed what one was required to believe with Supernatural Faith. But Catholic teaching rejects this idea. Consider what the Catechism says: "In *all* he says and does, man is *obliged* to follow faithfully what *he knows* to be just and right." (§1778) It does not say *"man need only follow faithfully what is just and right in those individual matters that the Catholic Church's Magisterium teaches are true."* Indeed, it is clear that "not required *as a matter of* Catholic Faith" must never be erroneously conflated with "never possibly an obligation of any sort for any Catholic."

Even beyond these considerations, however, we ought not be too quick to decide, in the first place, that a given matter is "only a private-revelation-matter." It is not as if a thing *being spoken of in* private revelations thereby qualifies it as "only" such a matter. On the contrary, when a certain truth becomes so repeated, over such a long period of time, by so many different saintly souls, then rejecting that truth merely because its impetus can be traced back to private revelations risks going far beyond simply rejecting a given private revelation. Rather, it strays into more dangerous territory still. For, as Catholics who rightly reject "Sola Scriptura," we know that the Word of God is more than what is written on the pages of the Bible, as it also includes *living* Sacred Tradition which flows "from the same divine wellspring…and [tends] toward the same end" as Scripture itself (*Dei Verbum* §8,9).

To reject the Gift—or Its universal Reign in the Era—is not merely to reject one or two private revelations; it is to claim that a fundamental tenet of 20th-century mysticism (including that of St. Faustina, Bl. Conchita, Bl. Dina Belanger, St. Maximilian Kolbe, St. Elizabeth of the Trinity, and many others—see Chapters 3 and 1) is a diabolical lie. And to assert that the Gates of Hell could be treated by the authority of the Church as these mystics and revelations have already, in fact, been treated by the same, is to come dangerously close to asserting that the Gates of Hell may have already succeeded in prevailing against the Church. But this, in turn, would call Our Lord a liar by virtue of His promise in Matthew 16:18. Restricting our focus to Luisa in particular, remember that if the Gift of Living in the Divine Will and the impending Reign of this Gift over the whole earth are wrong, then Luisa hasn't merely been mistaken on a few of her opinions. No, rather, *in that case her entire life-long (81-year) mission would have been a diabolical lie or a historically unprecedented fraud.* For we are always left with this simple dichotomy when it comes to claims of *such* great magnitude, *so* emphasized, *so* repeated, over *so* many years: either they are true, or they are from the Gates of Hell. Thus, it will not work to say, "clearly Luisa was a holy woman, but this 'Gift' and this 'Era' in her writings are simply not true." Such an assessment is rendered impossible by the same rational dichotomy that rightly denounces the lukewarm approach to Christ Himself; as many wise authors have demonstrated (especially C.S. Lewis), it is absurd to claim that Jesus "was a good and wise teacher, but certainly not Divine." For one who claims to *be* God either *is* God or is a lunatic (or a demon). In a similar way, the nature of Luisa's revelations, leave no room for the lukewarm diagnosis. An author, in some cases, may be separable from his work. A mystic, however, cannot be separated from her mysticism when this mysticism *was her entire life's purpose, for her entire life.*

Am I then asserting that those who fail to heed Luisa's revelations are damned to hell? Of course not. I pray that you, dear Catholics, above all remain always at peace despite any exhortations I have presented before you. (At the same time, I earnestly hope that whoever has bothered to open to this section has long ago moved on from that lamentable approach to the Faith which is concerned only with the bare-minimum requirements of squeezing his way into Heaven!)

Weren't Luisa's writings condemned on the Index of Forbidden Books?

Indeed, Luisa's revelations once were on the Index; right alongside St. Faustina's revelations—a placement that was emptied of all meaning upon the abolition of the Index by Pope St. Paul VI in 1966. This abolition obviously did not by itself magically render orthodox all the former contents of the Index, but it did mean that, from that point forward, no conclusions could be drawn from a given work merely having once been placed therein (recall that the condemnations of Luisa's writings were nullified by Cardinal Ratzinger—Pope Benedict XVI—in 1994).

By the logic of avoiding anything that was on the Index or was once condemned, we must not merely avoid Luisa and Faustina, but we must also have nothing to do with St. Joan of Arc, St. Teresa of Avila, St. Padre Pio, the approved apparitions of Our Lady of All Nations, Blaise Pascal, Copernicus, Victor Hugo, St. Athanasius, St. Mary MacKillop, and many other saints, valid revelations, edifying works, and factual treatises (but I will end the list here and spare you a review of all Church History!). Luisa's writings are no longer condemned. Clericalism evidently dies hard; still, some Catholics today refuse to realize that the Church's juridical actions are not infallible, and, indeed, they often change and, in so changing, reveal how wrong they were at first. **The only voices that count on this question (that is, the Vatican and Luisa's diocese of Trani in Italy) have repeatedly affirmed that the older condemnations are not binding, and, quite the contrary, that they earnestly desire Luisa's writings to be read and her spirituality to be lived.**

Aren't Luisa's revelations at least unapproved?

Luisa's revelations are in many ways approved, and in some ways are still awaiting full approval. Whoever dismisses them as "unapproved private revelations" is being partial at best; ignoring, for example, everything laid out in the relevant portion of Chapter I of this book. Granted, there is indeed a temporary and partial "Moratorium" limiting the open publication of the existing translations of Luisa's volumes (until the imminent release of the Official Edition of the same), but the nature of this Moratorium is completely distorted by certain individuals (and on certain websites) whose incorrect assertions are, tragically, often deferred to by well-meaning Catholics who make the mistake of trusting whatever a "Google search" first presents without digging any deeper. I have dealt with this matter thoroughly and honestly in pages 483-488 of *The Crown of Sanctity*, but for now, suffice it to say that *the very Archbishop from whom this Moratorium proceeds* was (he is now deceased) a zealous promoter and defender of Luisa's revelations, who specifically encouraged reading them! (He merely wished the writings to be shared among prayer groups wherein they can be properly explained; not yet openly published before the footnoted official edition's publication). So much for using his own juridical actions as a mark against Luisa's revelations.

But even if Luisa's revelations were entirely unapproved, that would be no mark against their glory; **every now-approved revelation was once unapproved, and only became approved because faithful souls were willing to nevertheless heed the call from Heaven contained therein.** Closing one's ears and heart to the "intrusion" of Heaven under the pretense of sticking with the apparent "safety" of heeding only that which is already fully approved is absurd—refuted by logic, refuted by Church History, and now even condemned the Church's Magisterium itself. In 2018, Pope Francis taught, in *Gaudete et Exsultate §170*, that the Church's "sound norms" are necessary, *but not sufficient* for discernment, and the Catechism teaches not that the faithful must await the Church's decisions on such matters, but rather the opposite—that the sense of the faithful *"knows* how to discern and welcome in these revelations whatever constitutes an authentic call of Christ…" (§67)

Now, obviously, we should always obey the Church. But this virtue of obedience says nothing about what we should do regarding matters on which the Church has not yet rendered a definitive verdict. As if to urge Catholics to not remain paralyzed, the Congregation for the Doctrine of Faith recently promulgated a document entitled "Norms regarding the manner of proceeding in the discernment of presumed apparitions or revelations." Published officially in English by the Vatican only several years ago, it gives the faithful the principles necessary to properly discern private revelations. Using these criteria, **we must trust that God's grace will allow us to discern His Will and we must proceed with courage.** If we are going to broadly and categorically reject this open-to-Heaven-approach, preferring instead to go about our spiritual lives with our tails tucked between our legs—ever paranoid that the devil is behind every rock—in hopes that this delusional "safety at all costs" strategy will give us peace, then why even be Christian at all? For that is precisely the pseudo- "peace" that Christ explicitly said He did *not* come to bring (cf. Matthew 10:34). One thing, dear friends, is certain: when Christ comes again, it will be entirely unapproved. I wish to close this section with more exhortations from Pope Francis' above quoted Magisterial Document in hopes that they inspire you to leave aside that lukewarm Christianity-lite approach to Heaven which always insists upon fearing anything not yet fully approved:

> "This should excite and encourage us to give our all and to embrace that unique plan that God willed for each of us from eternity." (§13) "Each saint is a mission, planned by the Father to reflect and embody, at a specific moment in history, a certain aspect of the Gospel." (§19) "Try to [live your entire life as a mission] by listening to God in prayer and recognizing the signs that he gives you." (§23) "God infinitely transcends us… we are not the ones to determine when and how we will encounter him." (§41) "It is not enough that everything be calm and peaceful. God may be offering us something more, but in our comfortable inadvertence, we do not recognize it." (§172)

Isn't this an artificial development with claims that are simply too extraordinary?

Although Luisa's writings do indeed contain the most glorious private revelations that Heaven has ever graced the Church with, nowhere within their thousands of pages is there any hint of dispensationalism, a claim to a new public revelation, or a claim to a surpassing of Public Revelation. **In each page, Luisa's writings present themselves as only a *private* revelation that is entirely subservient to—fitting within the framework of and** resting upon the foundation of—Public Revelation in Christ (the Deposit of Faith).

But we must address an elementary confusion of language that some have succumbed to regarding what the Church teaches on this matter: nowhere has the Church placed limits on how grand or glorious *of a claim private revelation may make*—the Church only teaches that a private revelation cannot claim to *itself* surpass or correct Public Revelation (cf. Catechism §67). For example; Mormonism, Jehovah's Witnesses, Christian Science, the "Palmarian Catholic Church," the "Army of Mary," and so many other movements and ideologies claim to be the recipients of revelations *which are themselves superior to* (or at least completing of and/or correcting) Public Revelation in Christ. The "Army of Mary," which claims to be Catholic, "moves on" from the Dogma of the Trinity for the sake of its newly "revealed" diabolical anti-Dogma of the "Quinternity." Similarly, the Palmarian "Catholic" Church pretends that its own "private revelation" bestows upon it the right to exceed the authority of the Church established by Christ and proceed to enthrone its own Pope. A few clearly false private revelations in the last several years have likewise erroneously claimed the authority to denounce the Pope or even claim he is the Antichrist. And I do not think there is any need for me to review how the other movements mentioned above likewise claim they have received revelations which surpass Public Revelation. (The Modernists are also prone to supposing that their insights are superior to Public Revelation—but, in even greater arrogance, it is usually pride in their own intellects and scholarship that they hold as supreme, as opposed to an alleged message from Heaven. Thus, to the thunderous applause of the world, they giddily contradict those Dogmas of the Church which they are proud of having "evolved" beyond.) But nowhere do Luisa's private revelations assert anything even remotely related to such claims. You will easily see this if you open their pages and read; but for now, a few comparisons will suffice. **In each of the following considerations, we will contrast, first, definitive Public Revelation in Christ vs. second, private revelation through Luisa:**

In Public Revelation, God is revealed as Three Persons, not One vs. In Luisa's private revelations, these Three Persons simply now wish to share Their life more fully. ·· In Public Revelation, Jesus reveals Himself as Divine vs. Luisa insists she is the lowliest of all creatures, and Jesus confirms she is just that. ·· In Public Revelation, a new, permanent Church is established on earth that is necessary for salvation vs. In Luisa's private revelations, a new *spirituality* is introduced, intended to be obedient to and peacefully fit within this same Church. ·· In Public Revelation, Seven Sacraments are instituted vs. In Luisa's private revelations, no Sacraments are instituted; the same Seven Sacraments remain the path to holiness. ·· In Public Revelation, a new Priesthood is established vs. In Luisa's private revelations, no new priesthood is formed: these very same (Catholic) priests are called to be the primary heralds of the Divine Will. ·· In Public Revelation, laws are altered (e.g. Divorce made impermissible, juridical Mosaic precepts dispensed from, all foods declared clean, circumcision abolished) vs. In Luisa's private revelations, the laws are entirely unchanged. ·· In Public Revelation, a radically new liturgy is instituted vs. In Luisa's private revelations, the liturgy is identical. ·· In Public Revelation, there is a total change in leadership away from the Levitical Priesthood and to the Petrine Ministry vs. In Luisa's private revelations, all authority remains with the Successor of Peter and all his Magisterium.

A clear picture emerges even from this brief consideration of some essentials of both

the Definitive Public Revelation we have been given *in* Christ, and the private revelations on the Divine Will we have been given *through* Luisa: they are entirely and un-confusedly distinct in nature. The revelations given to Luisa fit squarely within the boundaries of private revelation as given by the Church; boundaries which nevertheless in no way deprive such revelations of the right to *speak of* things that are even greater than Redemption itself. Redemption is the primary *concern and object* of Public Revelation's Deposit of Faith, but not synonymous for the same. *Any* private revelation which, for example, gives insights into the glories of Heaven is also *speaking of* something greater than this primary concern and object of Public Revelation's Deposit of Faith. For ends are always superior to their corresponding means, and Redemption is the *means* to the *end* of Heaven. This does *not* mean that the approved revelations to St. Catherine of Siena (or the so many more like them that reveal truths about Heaven) are thereby detracting from Public Revelation's superiority to private revelation. With this proper understanding of the relevant Church teachings, one realizes that Luisa's revelations, too—though they *speak of* an impending Third Fiat of Sanctification (the Era) that will in *some ways* surpass Redemption itself—are revelations that in no way, shape, or form claim *for themselves* a status that surpasses, corrects, or completes Public Revelation.

Jesus' revelations to Luisa do indeed make *enormous claims*. But **if there was ever any merit to the view (there never was) that private revelation has no right to do anything but sit quietly in a corner and make occasional polite suggestions about pious devotional practices, then that view was nevertheless demolished by the historically unprecedented degree of Church approval and exaltation given to St. Faustina's revelations** (which now no reasonable Catholic doubts, and which make claims of astounding magnitude). For Faustina's revelations claim to constitute *the* very preparation of the *world* for the Coming of Christ (§429), *demand* the institution of a new obligatory Liturgical Feast (Divine Mercy Sunday; §570) and the veneration by the Church Universal of a particular image (the Divine Mercy Image; §49), reveal with great clarity a new holiness (see Chapter 3), and even offer an absolute promise, unprecedented in all Church history, saying that the faithful undertaking of its requests will result in complete remission of all sin *and* punishment—a veritable second Baptism, for it does not entail the same requirements as a plenary indulgence (§300, §699)—among a multitude of other extraordinary claims.

The Catechism does not say that Public Revelation is "closed, ended, and fully understood." Rather, the Catechism simply states that Public Revelation is *"complete,"* and that no "new public revelation" is to be expected (§66). Taking the Catechism at its word, one sees that revelation is still unfolding—*not* in the sense that there will be any new public revelations, but in the sense that *the* Public Revelation we already have remains to be fully explicated, applied, and lived. *Private* revelation, in turn, is an indispensable part of this unfolding, which we artificially restrain only at our own peril.

"Christ's works do not go backwards but forwards," taught Pope Benedict XVI (General Audience. March 10, 2010), offering a well-placed rebuke of those who erroneously hold that, after the New Testament, Church History simply declines. And this rebuke is most clearly applicable to those who pretend that private revelation must never be too great. Accordingly, a discerning mind would *expect* private revelation to grow in glory as time goes on and we draw closer to Christ's Second Coming. The only truly strange thing would be if that were not so.

The job of the Magisterium of the Church is not to convey all the details of what is coming upon the world and the Church until the end of time. How easy it is to fall into the perennial trap of the Pharisee, yelling "heresy!" at any surprise. Against this, Pope Francis has repeatedly taught—both informally and officially—that God has many surprises in store for us, and that we have no right to close ourselves off to God's plans for the sake of the apparent security of our old ways of doing things. **But it was the traditionally-minded and pre-conciliar Venerable Pope Pius XII, and not Pope Francis, who most forcefully repudiated the novelty-phobic attitude; for he taught,** *in his high-level Magisterium,* **"... all moreover should** *abhor* **that intemperate zeal which imagines that whatever is new should for that very reason be opposed or suspected ..."** (*Divino Afflante Spiritu* §47)

Luisa's revelations fit beautifully on the foundation of Sacred Tradition, as we saw in Chapter 3. They are not, however, without their surprises for the Church. But that is nothing to lament; the Magisterium is a solid foundation on which to stand and a sure fence safeguarding the edge of a dangerous cliff—not a cage to lock oneself inside and hide within. **Far from being an artificial rupture in the development of Sacred Tradition, Luisa's revelations are the very definition and epitome of an organic development: for they speak of the moment when the flower blooms.** The bloom, of course, will surprise one who thought he was only observing the linear growth of a blade of grass, but how lamentable it would be for this observer to turn his surprise into a castigation of the flower! Everything has been leading up to this development *perfectly* and *beautifully*. (And the main thrust of this budding is seen everywhere in 20th-century mysticism). But this can only be recognized by one with an unclenched fist.

Isn't this holiness too great and too easy? What about St. Joseph?

Perhaps one protests to the Gift with the following words, *"It is absurd to say that we can now receive a new Gift of sanctity that, before the 20th century, only Jesus, Mary, Adam, and Eve had. What about St. Joseph? St. Francis? St. Augustine? St. Paul? Why now for so great a gift, given such great saints in Church History?"*

Now, either one *does*, or one does *not* believe in the existence of the Gift. If he does not believe that this Gift exists, how, then, can he pretend to be offended at the notion of the saints of previous times in the Church not having it? If, on the other hand, he *does* believe that the Gift exists, how can he be so foolish as to allow these pietistical concerns to prevent him from desiring and asking for such a great good? Nevertheless, we shall consider the concern. **Having a greater gift does not make its recipient "greater" than one who has not received it merely because the latter did not live in the time of that gift.** Accordingly, although the Eucharist is an infinitely greater gift than Moses ever received—you having received it does not make *you* greater than Moses. Confession is a greater gift than King David ever received—but your thus far received absolutions do not render *you* greater than he. Addressing the greatest of the saints listed in the objection above, it is clear that **St. Joseph always has been and always will be the greatest saint after the Blessed Virgin (cf. Leo XIII,** *Quamquam Pluries* §3**); Luisa's revelations make no attempt to alter that.** Jesus even tells Luisa that His Kingdom was in full force in the home of Nazareth and that Joseph fully lived in the reflections of the Divine Will in this home, and that Joseph was *the* prime minister of this Kingdom (cf. July 7, 1928)—a sovereign dignity not given even to Luisa. Whether Joseph was fully given the Gift Itself is not relevant to ascertaining *his* greatness. What *is* certain is that St. Joseph did not live in such a time as to allow him to receive the Eucharist, but the absence of this great gift from his life in no way detracts from his own greatness, and only a fool would castigate another who glorifies the Eucharist on account of this glorification allegedly detracting from the glory due to St. Joseph. Let us, however, broaden our scope and consider the more general "but why now?" protestation.

As Jesus said in the Gospel, "Are you envious because I am generous?" (Matthew 20:15) Adopting the attitude of one who is willing to complain, *"but why wouldn't God do it this other way?"* in response to what God—in His perfect plan and infinite wisdom—has deemed fitting, is a sure way of making grace run off of a soul like water off of a rock. Why didn't God reveal the Sacred Heart or Divine Mercy devotions earlier, perhaps to St. Mary Magdalene? Why weren't the Desert Fathers blessed with the Holy Rosary and its corresponding promises? Why was daily Communion not broadly encouraged before the reign of Pope St. Pius X in the 20th century? Why weren't seven-year-olds permitted to receive before that same reign? **God has predetermined His timeline, and it is not ours to question. It is only ours to ask, when an alleged revelation or development comes along, *"is this from God?"* If it is from God, then we must bend the knee and unclench the fist.**

Whoever remains concerned that the Gift is "too easy" should remember that the *entire first third* of Luisa's volumes consists in a beautiful exposition of (and exhortation to) the traditional three stages of the spiritual life (the Purgative, Illuminative, and Unitive). Her writings *build* on this foundation of Sacred Tradition; they do not repudiate it. This criticism makes as much sense as opening the Bible at random and, upon reading of the Incarnation, repudiating God for not first preparing well the way with prophets and a moral law.

Now, in considering the ontological possibility of the Gift, all must acknowledge that God is at least certainly *capable* of working the same type of holiness in anyone that He has already worked in the Blessed Virgin. Indeed, the Blessed Virgin Mary is the greatest creature that will ever exist (*far* greater than *anyone else* who has the Gift), but we must nevertheless acknowledge that Our Lady is a creature, thus whatever *type of holiness* she enjoys has been entirely given to her by God, and whatever type of holiness God gave to her, He is also capable of giving to others. There are simply no Magisterial, theological, Scriptural, philosophical, or any other grounds for denying this ontological possibility. **In Mary, God showed us all what He is capable of doing in a human being. If He can give something to Mary, then He can give it to us**; we who are her children and who are no more or less human than she is, and whom she—more than any other creature—desires to become recipients of her own Gift. Since no one can deny this, all one can do to oppose the Gift is to castigate God for His imprudence in being so generous with His grace in these days where "sin abounds."(cf. Romans 5:20) We needn't spend any time here refuting the absurdity of placing oneself in that position!

But even if we leave aside all that has been stated above, the criticisms that the sanctity of Living in the Divine Will revealed in Luisa's writing is "too great" because it is higher even than spiritual marriage, or "too easy" because it is based primarily on sincere desire for the Gift, are both illicit on the sole grounds that they could be equally levied against

St. Thérèse of Lisieux, St. Faustina, Blessed Conchita, St. Elizabeth of the Trinity, and a multitude of mystics of the 20th century; many of whom are now Beatified or Canonized (see Chapter 3).

We must remember that nothing in Luisa's revelations is a mark against the singular privileges enjoyed by Our Lady. Jesus repeatedly makes it clear to Luisa that she is no Virgin Mary—that the Blessed Virgin, *not* Luisa, is the Queen of the Divine Will, and that Luisa will never come close to this Queen (nor will any of us). Jesus even laments to Luisa that people had, in her own day, falsely accused the messages of conflating Luisa and Mary:

> They spoke as if I had told you that you were as though another Queen. How much nonsense-I did not say that you are like the Celestial Queen, but that I want you similar to Her, just as I have said to many other souls dear to Me that I wanted them similar to Me; but with this they would not become God like Me. (May 19, 1931)

On the other hand, it is true that Luisa is the "earthly head" of this mission of the Third Fiat of Sanctification. But what is so difficult to believe about that? In this mission, Jesus needs to use a human instrument who is still a wayfarer, as He always does in His greatest works. Is it surprising that He chose a lowly, ordinary, virgin?

Some, however, have the very opposite objection to the one stated above; they hold that this holiness revealed to Luisa is too *small*. For, they say, Christian holiness is *already* greater than Adam's prelapsarian holiness in every way. But they are wrong; the Fathers of the Church starkly contradict this view (teaching, for example, that prelapsarian Adam's *very life principle itself* was none other than the Holy Spirit), and even Aquinas points out that there are *two* ways in which Adam's holiness is greater than Christian holiness, and only *one* way in which Christian holiness is greater (cf. *Summa Theologica* First Part, Question 95, Article 4). Although the Catechism (cf. §375) does imply that Christian Holiness surpasses original holiness in one sense, Jesus affirms the same to Luisa (see Chapter 4), and, furthermore, the Church teaches elsewhere that original holiness was in another way greater than Christian holiness (e.g. the Liturgical Prayer, "you *call* human nature back to its original holiness," meaning, as all "calls" do, that even one with Christian holiness must strive after—which always implies working towards something still greater—original holiness). This concern, however, can only be adequately addressed within the context of God's overarching plan with history itself, which we considered in the "Story of History: Redux" section, and which should be consulted by anyone interested in the matter.

Isn't this Millenarianism?

In perfect agreement with the Popes since Leo XIII and the multitudes of trustworthy revelations prophesying the Era (some of which were discussed in Chapter 1), Luisa's revelations not only *do not* teach Millenarianism, modified Millenarianism, or anything of the sort, but they also *specifically repudiate these errors* (and all the errors listed in the next paragraph that are associated with them). For example, regarding the error that Jesus will physically reign on earth—He tells Luisa the Era will be a *Sacramental* reign in *grace* (cf. November 2, 1926). Regarding the error that there will be a "rapture"—He tells Luisa that, even if many souls in grace are protected, they nevertheless will have to live through the Chastisements on earth (a constant theme in these revelations). Regarding the error that the "age of the Church," along with its hierarchies and doctrines, will pass away for the sake of the "age of the Spirit"—He tells Luisa the opposite; namely, that the Era consists in the Church acquiring her *full vigor*, not passing away (cf. September 2, 1901), and that *Catholic priests* will be its primary heralds (cf. January 13, 1929). Regarding the error that the Eternal Resurrection of the Dead will occur before the Era—He tells Luisa that there *will* be death during the Era, and the bodies of those who die during the Era will, in their sepulchers, *await* the Day of the Resurrection (cf. October 22, 1926). Regarding the error that the Beatific Vision will be enjoyed on earth and Faith no longer needed—He tells Luisa there will still be the need for Faith, although it will be much clearer than it generally is today (cf. June 29, 1928). Regarding the error that those in the Era will be ontologically confirmed in grace and categorically incapable of any sort of sin or suffering—He says that only in Heaven does such ontological confirmation exist (cf. September 29, 1931) and that even in the Era, there can be suffering, although of a triumphant and glorious nature (cf. August 22, 1926).

There are nine erroneous ideologies—some condemned heresies, others simply mistaken notions—each of which the Era is occasionally tragically confused with, and each of which must be zealously avoided: 1) Standard Millenarianism (Montanus/Chiliasm). 2) Modified Millenarianism. 3) Hedonistic Millenarianism (Cerinthus—incidentally, the only type of Millenarianism St. Augustine famously condemned) 4) The Spiritual Legacy of Joachim of Fiore. 5) Dispensationalism. 6) Progressive Evolutionism. 7) Secular Messianism. 8) Liberation Theology. 9) Utopianism. **Each of these errors is light-years apart from the anticipations of the Era unanimously agreed upon by trustworthy private revelations (above all, those given to Luisa).** Unfortunately, though, there are a few authors today who have published their own Era-free eschatological speculations, and who systematically distort Scripture, Magisterium, and private revelation to try and popularize a false appearance in which the Era seems to be the heresy of modified Millenarianism. But **the Church's own authority has already defined even *modified* Millenarianism as consisting in the anticipation of Christ *physically* reigning on earth** (full blown *un*-modified Millenarianism, on the other hand, includes additional errors beyond this; e.g. the rapture, a pre-Era Eternal Resurrection, the Beatific Vision and definitive perfection of man on earth). For example, the July 21, 1944 Declaration of the Holy Office specifically defines modified Millenarianism as the system of teachings wherein Christ "will come visibly to rule over this world." (*Acta Apostolica Sedis*. Annus XXXVI – Series II – Vol. XI. Page 212) The mere fact the Era's critics are attempting to supersede the authority of the Church by defining "modified" on their own terms, in contradiction to how the Church has already done, should immediately tell any orthodox Catholic that these people should not be credited. Due, however, to the sheer quantity (not quality—which is incredibly low) and popularity (in a few circles) of their arguments, I dedicated an entire chapter to refuting their distortions in *The Crown of Sanctity*, and I encourage anyone who has been exposed to their positions to read it (pages 356-396).

Recall that, in the book, *Our Father: Reflections on the Lord's Prayer*, Pope Francis teaches, "The kingdom of God is here *and* [emphasis in original] the kingdom of God will come... the kingdom of God is coming now but at the same time has not yet come completely..." In perfect accord with Catholic teaching, Jesus' message to Luisa is this:

the time has now arrived for the Kingdom He preached 2,000 years ago to arrive more fully on earth than it ever has before. **This is fully orthodox and should be overwhelmingly exciting to all Catholics. Do not, dear readers, let certain thieves of hope who preach an Eschatology of Despair convince you otherwise.**

Isn't this the heresy of Monothelitism or Quietism?

Luisa's revelations repeatedly teach the opposite of Monothelitism: Jesus tells Luisa that He *did* have a human will, and that He wants our wills *little* (just as St. Thérèse of Lisieux taught)—not annihilated; *active* (with His very own activity)—not passive. Nowhere do Luisa's writings either teach or imply any of the 43 propositions that the Church has condemned as the heresy of Quietism (cf. *Coelestis Pastor*, Pope Innocent XI, 1687). **Throughout Luisa's volumes we see the opposite of Quietism relentlessly taught:** moral effort being paramount, salvation and (avoiding) Purgatory being extremely important, interceding for others encouraged, lamenting the loss of souls (and other evils), firm insistence on all the virtues traditionally upheld, praying for mitigation of chastisements, etc. **Any allegations of Quietism could be far more easily levied against the many saints, Doctors of the Church, and other mystics quoted in Chapter 3 of this book—and any allegedly "Quietistic" elements in Luisa's writings are found far more explicitly in these works of unassailable orthodoxy.** In the following excerpts from Luisa's writings, and so many others like them, we see clearly refuted any hint of Quietism, Monothelitism (or any corollary thereof), etc.:

> [Jesus says:] I had a human will which had not even one breath of life, surrendering the place to my Divine Will in everything... (July 19, 1928) Without destroying anything of what the creature does...[My Divine Will] animates them with Its light, It embellishes them, and communicates to them Its Divine Power. (September 16, 1931) My daughter, the human will *on its own* is nauseating, *but united with Mine is the most beautiful thing I created.* (January 31, 1928) [Luisa wrote, expounding upon Jesus' revelations to her:] ...nor does Jesus want [my will] to be completely destroyed. He wants it yet small, but alive, so as to be able to operate inside a living will, not a dead one, to be able to have His small little field of action within my littleness, which, being small, incapable, weak, with reason must lend itself to receive the great operating of the Divine Fiat. (March 26, 1933)

Expanding our consideration of this concern, we can also see that Pantheism, Hinduism, and Buddhism teach a spirituality radically distinct from Luisa's revelations; for these religions and philosophies teach that one need only *recognize* the "identity or sameness of the Atman—the deepest self—with the Brahman—the Godhead" (Hinduism), or the "Godhead of everything" (Pantheism), or the "extinguishment or nirvana of the self" (Buddhism). Luisa's revelations teach not the extinguishing of the self, but the sacrificing of the self-will to God. They teach not the "recognition" of the divinity of the self, but the *attainment* of the divinization of the self through the ordinary Catholic spiritual life, *combined with* desiring the Gift of Living in the Divine Will. They teach not the Divinity *of* all things, but the Divine *impression left on* all created things by their Divine Craftsman and how these things serve as *veils of* (not literal incarnations of) the Divine Will.

What is all this talk about 6,000 years? What about evolution and geology?

Nowhere in Luisa's revelations is either evolution or young earth creationism spoken of—on these questions, all that one *must* believe in order to remain consistent with

Luisa's revelations is that Adam and Eve are indeed our first parents and that they did indeed fall from grace about 6,000 years ago (although I propose that one go much further than that in rejecting the modern view on these matters; see *The Crown of Sanctity* pages 526-532). If even that appears too tall an order, bear in mind that the Catholic Faith essentially requires as much. In *Humani Generis §37*, Pope Pius XII authoritatively condemned the notion that humanity proceeds from more than one set of parents (Adam and Eve). Furthermore, even if much of the Book of Genesis is merely symbolic (although the same Encyclical also teaches that Genesis does indeed pertain to history in the true sense, cf. §38), the genealogy in the Gospel of Luke makes it impossible to claim that there are tens-of-thousands (much less hundreds-of-thousands) of years standing between the present day and Adam and Eve's begetting of their first son, Cain.

✳✳✳

A final note on the concerns of Catholics. As a teacher myself, I am as tempted as anyone is to take the erroneous approach to mysticism—thus, I feel I must repeat what I must often remind myself: mysticism ought never be approached as a theology professor approaches grading a student's term paper. Mysticism is not primarily an intellectual exercise. It must be judged above all by its fruits, and its various literary forms (and the *mode of the receiver*) must be understood and considered, so that what the text *actually means* can be received in accordance with God's intended purpose. What would become of the entire 2,000-year history of the Catholic Spiritual Tradition if a quibbling, literalistic, rationalistic, hair-splitting, obsessive-compulsive approach was taken to mysticism? It would be in shambles, and our glorious Faith would have devolved into a mere philosophy (as Pope Francis rightly so labels religion without mysticism). If I were a dishonest man, I would surreptitiously send Luisa's critics copies of selections of works by St. Francis de Sales, St. Faustina, St. Maximilian Kolbe, St. Hildegard, St. Elizabeth of the Trinity, St. Thérèse of Lisieux, and the Greek Fathers of the Church—claiming they were written by Luisa, and asking for responses. And do you know what would happen? Rest assured that I would receive long treatises written by these critics, detailing all sorts of "doctrinal errors" they found in these works, so exalted by the Church, which they thought were from Luisa. Thankfully for the critics, however, I am not a dishonest man.

†‡†

Detailed Contents

Endnotes

[1] *Jesus Christ Bearer of the Water of Life*, 1.5.

[2] Considering the indefinite article and the contrasting references in the following chapter of his book, this is clearly not a literal reference to the actual *Eternal* Resurrection of which the Creed speaks.

[3] Justin understands this to be symbolic and is not insisting on a literal 1,000-year duration.

[4] cf. Peter Seewald. *Salt of the Earth: The Church at the End of the Millennium*. Pages 237-8.

[5] *Preparation for Total Consecration to Jesus through Mary for Families*. Page 192.

[6] "5 Saturdays, 1 Salvation." Joseph Pronechan. National Catholic Register. Oct 9, 2005

[7] Fr. Marie-Michel Philipon, O.P. *CONCHITA: A Mother's Spiritual Diary*. Misc. excerpts.

[8] cf. http://www.ncregister.com/blog/joseph-pronechen/major-apparitions-of-st.-joseph-are-approved

[9] Fr. Benedict Calvi, Luisa's final confessor appointed by the Church, even wrote: "What was her food? Everything she had eaten, after a few hours, came back up completely intact. All of [the mystical phenomena] I observed, scrupulously controlled and subjected to careful examination by many doctors and professors of dogmatic, moral, ascetic and mystical theology ..." (Quoted in Rev Joseph Iannuzzi's Doctoral Thesis., 1.8)

[10] Letter of St. Hannibal to Luisa Piccarreta, dated February 14th, 1927.

[11] Bernardino Giuseppe Bucci, OFM: *Luisa Piccarreta, A Collection of* Memories (Roma 52, San Ferdinando Di Puglia: Tipolitographia Miulli, 2000), Ch. 4.

[12] Address of Pope John Paul II to the Rogationist Fathers. Paragraph 6. 16 May 1997.

[13] Rev. Joseph L. Iannuzzi, Missionaries of the Most Holy Trinity Newsletter (Nov. 2014-May 2015): Page 2.

[14] En.luisapiccarretaofficial.org/news/the-miracle-attributed-to-luisa/44

[15] Which, contrary to a few frantically promoted rumors that Faustina's condemnation was nothing but a translation misunderstanding, was also clearly due to the enormity of the claims in Faustina's now fully approved revelations. (cf. John Allen Jr. "A saint despite Vatican reservations" August 30, 2002)

[16] H.G. Wells. "The War That Will End War," The Daily News. August 14, 1914

[17] Cf. St. Louis de Montfort. *True Devotion to Mary*. Paragraph 63.

[18] Nota Bene: when, in Luke 12, Jesus admonishes us to "fear him who… has authority to throw you into hell," He is not referring to the devil. The devil has no authority to throw us into hell; only our self-will can do that – the only thing worth "fearing." But since no one really fears himself in the sense of "fear" that I am here speaking, it can also be legitimately said that we ought to fear nothing.

[19] Cardinal Christoph Schonborn. *From Death to Life: The Christian Journey*. 1995. Page 50.

[20] Hugh Owen. *New and Divine: The holiness of the third Christian millennium*. John Paul II Institute of Christian Spirituality. 2001. p.44-45.

[21] Translated from the Italian of St. Maximilian's letters by the editors at Saintmaximiliankolbe.com

[22] Fr. Peter Fehlner. *St. Maximilian Kolbe: Martyr of Charity–Pneumatologist*. P. 37-9.

[23] Whereas, although the Gift is certainly in Faustina's writings discussed above, the main thrust of her Diary is the Divine Mercy, not the Divine Will.

[24] Fr. Marie-Michel Philipon, O.P. *CONCHITA: A Mother's Spiritual Diary*. Pages 57-58.

[25] Arthur Calkins. Missio Magazine. "The Venerable Conchita (Concepción Cabrera de Armida)—Part I"

[26] Rev. Joseph Iannuzzi. *The Splendor of Creation*. Ch. 3

[27] (ST, vol. & no.1, p. 36). Quoted in *Listen to My Prophets*. Fr. Edward O'Connor. P. 134.

[28] Blessed Dina Belanger, *The Autobiography of Dina Belanger*, translated by Mary St. Stephen, R.J.M. (Sillery: Religious of Jesus and Mary, 3rd edition, 1997), P. 219. (February 22, 1925). Cited in *New and Divine*.

[29] Bl. Dina Belanger, quoted in *New and Divine*. Hugh Owen. P. 85-91. Misc. excerpts.

[30] S. Ákerman (auth.), John Christian Laursen, Richard H. Popkin (eds.)-Millenarianism and Messianism.

[31] National Catholic Register. *Fatima's Sister Lucia Explains Why the Daily Rosary is a 'Must'* November 19, 2017. Joseph Pronechen.

Epilogue for Skeptics

So, you think I'm wrong... (Of course, this isn't about me. But I know that some readers simply will not allow in their minds an analysis that separates the matter at hand from the man presenting it. Therefore, to humor them, I will here briefly engage in a little Pauline folly (cf. 2 Corinthians 11), even though I am indeed the least worthy of all men whom God could have asked to engage in this mission of promoting the Divine Will.)

But What if I'm right? What if, indeed, the world is on the cusp of such a radical transformation that all the anxieties which now incessantly crowd your mind are about to die away like the jabbering of monkeys upon the entrance of a roaring lion? What if all that now worries and depresses you is about to melt away like a dream upon the blessed intrusion of a new reality you hitherto scarcely could have comprehended? What if, indeed, you were invited to not only know of this impending transformation, but to be on the right side of it and to be among the few who shall be forever remembered as its heralds?

Unlike the salesmen who employ a familiar strategy by ending their pitches in a similar manner, I have nothing to gain from you, and I ask nothing of you for myself. I will never start a "Divine Will Secrets Club" that you can join for a mere three easy payments of $99.99. Nor am I offering you a "deal you cannot refuse" by presenting snake oil before you and pleading with you to spare a few hundred dollars on account of the juxtaposed relatively minimal cost and apparently great rewards. I am, rather, a philosopher—a scholar and a professor whose *job* is to discover the truth, to *know* that it is the truth, to know *that* I know that it is the truth, to know *why* I know that it is the truth; all using only the most absolutely trustworthy logical methods and bulletproof reasoning in the process—who is offering you the very thing he has, over years of study and inquiry, become more convicted of than anything. And it just so happens that this something being offered to you will give both you and the world everything you could have ever legitimately hoped and dreamed for... *and all you have to do is want it and ask for it.*

Even if you have read this entire book and somehow remain unconvinced—is there anywhere to be found a more accurate definition of insanity than refusing this offer? All your life, you have had to move on from beliefs that you wished were true; beliefs that you so very much wanted to be true, but simply were not true. Here, at last, is something that no good man in his right mind could *not* want to be true—*and it is true.* **Not only is it true; it is supremely simple and merely confirms and strengthens what has always been the essence of your Faith—it is none other than praying *the greatest petition* of *the greatest prayer* with full faith and confidence that it really can be fulfilled in the greatest possible way. Why not do so? *Why not* trust that the Son of God will make good on His greatest promise? *Why not?***

And so...What if I'm wrong? Then both the world and your own life will still greatly benefit from heeding the admonitions and invitations presented within these pages.

But ... *what if I'm right?*

Then this is everything.

†‡†

Perhaps, however, you are not a skeptic; perhaps you're just someone who has turned directly to the end of this book in hopes of jumping straight to its conclusion! I wrote this book attempting to compress the essence of my earlier book, *The Crown of Sanctity*, into a vastly smaller package. But if you insist, I will acquiesce and strive to consolidate the moral of the story further still. Heed, then, at least this one brief exhortation.

I assume you would like a glorious Era of Peace to dawn upon the world soon. Well, this will require something of you. It will require that you make a commitment. So commit now—with all your heart and strength—to say one Our Father every single day for the rest of your life.

You hesitate. I understand. Such a commitment is a serious thing. But the word "absurd" should have as its very definition the refusal to make this particular commitment. It demands only 19 seconds of each day's 86,400. It consists merely in praying daily *the one and only prayer* which the Son of God Himself taught while He was on earth. I'm not, however, asking this only of Christians; I'm *imploring* it of every single human being on the face of the planet: whether Christian, Pagan, Hindu, Buddhist, Jew, Muslim, Atheist, Agnostic, or anything in between. Because whoever you are, you can at least acknowledge that Jesus is a man like no other to have ever walked the face of the planet, and at the absolute bare-bones-minimum, you clearly ought to at least pray daily the one prayer that stands out like the sun among all other prayers—**you truly must at least pray daily the one prayer which History's Only Unparalleled Man commanded us to pray.**

Imagine if a trustworthy company or government decided to offer complete insurance—health, car, house, life, etc.—to anyone who wanted it, at the cost of only a few pennies, and with no strings attached. Suppose there was not even the obligation to abandon one's insurance coverages he already has. Suppose, furthermore, this complete insurance could be purchased in secrecy, with no other obligations whatsoever. Perhaps for some reason you doubt that this institution, despite its trustworthiness, will make good on its promises. But you still would be insane to not spend the few pennies to purchase this plan. Indeed, I am certain that, if ever such an offer were to be made, you would immediately sign up. With Christ, we have something infinitely superior to this or any other analogy or illustration we could ever consider. We have God Himself in the flesh. And if only you give this simple *Fiat*—if only you pray one Our Father each day, with sincerity and full Faith that its promises really can be fulfilled in the greatest possible way, then I believe that this will put you on the right side of the Era.

It's worth it. Do not delay. Make the commitment.

†‡†

Our Father, Who art in Heaven, hallowed be Thy Name.
Thy Kingdom come. Thy Will be done, on earth as it is in Heaven.
Give us this day our daily bread, and forgive us our trespasses,
as we forgive those who trespass against us,
and lead us not into temptation,
but deliver us from evil.
Amen.

†‡†

Made in the USA
Monee, IL
07 June 2020